"IF PRESENT RATES OF CHILDBEARING, DIVORCE AND REMARRIAGE CONTINUE, AS MANY AS HALF OF TODAY'S CHILDREN COULD BE INVOLVED IN A STEPFAMILY AS CHILD OR PARENT SOMETIME IN THEIR LIVES."

—*The Wall Street Journal*

Already an estimated eight million children in America now live in stepfamilies. And if they are frequently bewildered and beleaguered in this new situation, so too are their stepparents.

Both the long-term relationship of stepparent to stepchild, and the day-to-day problems that must be overcome, require clear examination and straight-forward advice.

That is why this book was written—and why it should be read.

HOW TO SUCCEED AS A STEPPARENT

PETER G. JOLIN, MSW, CSW, PC is a professional counselor and psychotherapist practicing in Houston, Texas. Director of the Marriage and Divorce Counseling Center of Houston, he is an expert on matters relating to stepparenting and second families. Twice married, he brings a special sensitivity to his years of successful professional work with stepparents and their families.

HOW TO SUCCEED AS A STEPPARENT

by
Peter G. Jolin, MSW

A SIGNET BOOK

NEW AMERICAN LIBRARY

NAL BOOKS ARE AVAILABLE AT QUANTITY DISCOUNTS
WHEN USED TO PROMOTE PRODUCTS OR SERVICES. FOR
INFORMATION PLEASE WRITE TO PREMIUM MARKETING
DIVISION, NEW AMERICAN LIBRARY, 1633 BROADWAY,
NEW YORK, NEW YORK 10019.

Published by arrangement with the author. For information address
New American Library.

First Signet Printing, December, 1983

    3   4   5   6   7   8   9

SIGNET, SIGNET CLASSIC, MENTOR, PLUME, MERIDIAN
and NAL BOOKS are published in Canada by The New American
Library of Canada, Limited, Scarborough, Ontario

PRINTED IN CANADA

DEDICATION

This book is dedicated to the hundreds of step-parents and their families who have inspired my belief and confidence in the ability of people to find personal happiness and live well with others.

ACKNOWLEDGMENT

This is my first book. It would hardly have been done at all without the help of Rosalva Reyes-Hada who has been responsible for its design and production, and Mark Carpenter, who edited it to make it readable.

To Becky

CONTENTS

Chapter 1

GREAT EXPECTATIONS
DIE HARD

The American Dream

Most stepparents-to-be anticipate their role of parenthood with enthusiasm. They have a genuine willingness, even eagerness, to love and care for their stepchildren as if the children were their own flesh and blood. They see the children as part of a package with the adult they are marrying. Because they enjoy a warm relationship with the real parent, they assume that a loving relationship with the children will naturally follow.

There is sometimes a bit of self-congratulation, even smugness, at the prospect of beating the system. Here is an opportunity to have an instant family, to take on the mantle of responsible parenthood without having to go through the hassles of all the preliminaries. Some stepparents daydream of happy family outings to show off the children to friends or newly acquired grandparents. Norman Rockwell visions of Home Sweet Home lead some to be believe that they have entered the mainstream of American respectability. A loving home and family are still very much at the center of the American Dream.

For many, this is precisely what happens. With only minor periods of adjustment and the good will of all, new family structures evolve into rewarding relationships. For those who manage the transition smoothly, congratulations are in order. They are blessed greatly.

The American Nightmare

But for many others, high expectations are cruelly shattered. Instead of planning happy family functions, some stepparents find themselves struggling doggedly for some hope of emotional survival or just a few moments of peace. In the worst cases, stepparents may wish a certain child, or children, had never been born. Some fantasize playground or schoolbus accidents and funerals with small coffins. One woman reported a recurring fantasy of a raging house fire in which her three stepchildren were consumed, while she ran off to phone her sister and happily announce her liberation.

Of course, most fantasies are not so macabre; still, they have in common a hope that magically, if not catastrophically, the offending youngsters will disappear.

Fantasy And Guilt

In and of themselves, these fantasies are harmless. They are seldom even mentioned to the spouse or the children. What is harmful is the tremendous sense of guilt these fantasies engender in stepparents. Men and women who all their lives have been reasonably sure of their goodness and humanity find themselves contemplating heinous events. The occurrence of these fantasies shakes their basic beliefs in themselves. Guiltladen, fearing for both themselves and the children with a fear as irrational as the fantasies themselves, these folks often withdraw to a silent and painful emotional distance from everyone else in the household. Withdrawal produces its own sense of guilt when the stepparent preceives it as a cowardly retreat from the struggle to form normal and productive relationships in a family.

Guilt Compounded

So there is guilt. Guilt for being unable to love certain children. Guilt compounded by unbidden, unmanageable rage. Guilt compounded further by occasions when the rage erupts into verbal or physical lashing out at the children. And the guilt only deepens when it is turned inward at the self, even though that seems to be the only way to hold it in check.

At times, a stepparent's entire internal world may be engulfed in a maelstrom of rage and guilt. Beleaguered by real or imagined demands from their families for tenderness and loving, they can find none to give, all their energies being sapped in an effort to keep their rage in check.

A Source of Guilt: *The Primitive Voice*

The guilt derives from a cold, objective sureness that children should be loved, succored, and, above all, wanted. There is a primitive voice in all of us that demands the furtherance of the race. That voice convinces us that the highest statement of our humanity is a natural, spontaneous desire for the welfare of children. It tantalizes us with the promise that, through children, we will find true joy and meaning in our lives.

Whether that voice speaks truthfully is an open question. Nevertheless, its message is forcefully supported by thousand of years of scriptural interpretation, secular philosophies, and mythologies. An adult who looks at a child only to feel hostility and inexpressible rage must necessarily feel out of step with the rest of humankind. To admit to the feelings seems tantamount to a resignation from honorable human existence, a branding of oneself as unfit for companionship, understanding, and love.

A Source of Guilt: *Early Family Conditioning*

Unhappy relationships in stepparented families often have their cause, and their ultimate resolution, in the early expectations of both the stepparent and the natural parent spouse. These expectations arise from the beliefs each individual holds about the nature and purpose of the family. Beliefs about family are so fundamentally a part of a person's emotional makeup that even he may not be able to define them. Yet, they generate expectations from the moment he contemplates marriage.

You, from the time of birth, have a unique experience with your family of origin. Even as an infant, you quickly developed an awareness of how best to get other members of your family to meet your needs. If crying loudly produced food and dry comfort, you cried loudly. If cooing and gurgling accomplished your purpose faster, you cooed and gurgled. At the age of two or three, you learned to differentiate between members of your family, and you learned to differentiate between what could and could not be expected from each.

Thus you began to learn about roles in families.

15

Perhaps your father could only be approached with smiles and silence, so you may have generalized that fathers must be people who are not to be bothered with childish troubles. Mother would give stern lectures about carelessness while she bandaged a minor hurt, so all mothers must be people who deride the incompetence of children. Big brother was always good for a hug and a horseback ride, so all older brothers must be people who naturally care for younger siblings. Big sister could not be approached at all, so older sisters must be people who have no natural responsibilities in families.

Getting The Message

In your family or origin, you had no choice but to accept as natural and right the configuration of roles and responsibilities within your particular family. For many years, as you were growing up, there was no other frame of reference. Adults and older siblings wielded tremendous influence over your understanding of family roles. Their abilities so far exceeded yours as to seem almost godlike. Who could resist belief in the rightness of such creatures.

The main message from adults to their young children is the authoritarian message: "Since I am bigger than you, all I do, say, and think is right. I am to be obeyed and emulated." Sometimes the message is implied; sometimes it is made clearly, briefly, and forcefully explicit: "Because I am your father. Period."

Most other messages from parents are not so explicit and clear; rather, the child is left to interpret their meaning. Whether or not the child construes a message correctly, his interpretation takes on the same gospel quality as the authoritarian message, and he accepts it on the same basis. The child who experiences repeated whippings may surmise that whipping is the proper way for adults to treat children. The next generation gets whipped, too. The child who notices a parent getting drunk regularly, but hears the parent saying drinking is evil, may surmise it is okay to get drunk as long as he feels guilty about it.

The list of messages you've accepted from your family of origin is endless. Some are positive, some are negative.

The Difficulty of Examining Old Assumptions

The ambiguous nature of early messages makes them, in later years, hard to sort out and examine for truth and usefulness. Because their intent or meaning is implied, they work subtle effects on the child's mind, and their very ambiguity makes them extremely difficult to grapple with in any forthright way.

Some messages seem to be contradictory, especially those related to dealings with other people or to the family itself. For example, there are ambiguous, yet forceful, demands to accept the emotional, intellectual, and physical limits of others; yet, the child's own limits are overlooked. Or, the child may receive an unambiguous message that families are good, along with an equally powerful, but implied, demand that no one dare ask why they are good.

As adults we believe, at least in principle, that we have a right to question and examine anything that comes to hand. As a matter of practice, however, we seldom undertake a critical examination of our own values and beliefs. Old, powerful, family prohibitions operate against such examinations. On top of that, there are equally powerful prohibitions against examining the prohibitions themselves.

Even if we were emotionally and intellectually free enough to probe into our basic beliefs, it's hard to ask the right questions. Familial messages, having been accepted, turn into inarticulate assumptions about the proper nature and form of family relationships. These assumptions manifest themselves in behavior and attitudes. To the extent that the early messages were ambiguous, so are the assumptions derived from them, so that behavior in relationships becomes fuzzy and often misdirected.

The First Step

Your success at stepparenting ultimately rests on your ability to clarify and appraise—with objectivity and brutal frankness—your beliefs about the value, nature, form, and purpose of a family. These beliefs must then be compared to an equally honest appraisal of beliefs held by your spouse, the natural parent.

This process of clarifying and appraising your beliefs about the concept of family will help you decide how you need to be treated. This may sound as if it should require very little thought, but, be assured, it is a complex matter. Knowing how you must be treated, knowing what your needs are—this is a first step, and a necessary one, before those to follow can be useful.

You must ask the right questions before you can get meaningful answers. The answers may not be to your, or your spouse's, liking. But if they are honest, they are meaningful, and you have achieved an opportunity for real understanding between you. This can be a tough, sometimes scary process, but, in the long run, it's worth it.

* * *

The following series of discussion questions are designed to help you and your mate better understand each other's ideas and beliefs about the families from which you came, and the one you are developing. If you use them conscientiously and thoroughly, they will help you greatly in establishing your position in your marriage and family.

DISCUSSION QUESTIONS

It will be best if the two of you can arrange a couple of hours of uninterrupted time for three or four sessions over a period of a week or two. Your responses to the questions should be as expansive and detailed as possible. If you ramble a little, that is all right. The whole idea is to think out loud and say your perceptions, clarify your own thinking, and help your partner understand. You may want to go through the whole series one at a time, or alternate your responses to each question. Do whatever is most comfortable for you. If a stepparent was significantly involved in your upbringing, apply responses to that person as well.

Both your mother and your father had significant influence on who you are today.
1. Who had the most influence? In what ways?
2. What about the other parent. How was his or her influence different?

3. How did your father show affection for you?

4. How did your mother show affection for you?

5. How did each of them show disapproval or punish you?

6. What kinds of things did your father especially appreciate in you when you were young?

7. What about your mother? Same question.

8. What kinds of things did your respective parents especially disapprove of in you when you were young?

9. Is your mother satisfied with the way you have turned out as an adult? If so why? If not, why not?

10. What about your father? Same question.

11. How would you characterize the relationship between your mother and father? (Note: If a stepparent was significantly involved in your upbringing, apply responses to that person as well).

12. How did your parents show affection for one another?

13. How did they fight?

14. How would you characterize your present relationship with your father? Are you satisfied with this relationship? Why?

15. How would you characterize your present relationship with your mother? Are you satisfied with this relationship? Why?

16. What are the three most important things of a positive nature you learned from your mother?
17. What about your father? Same question.
18. What are the three most important things of a negative nature you learned from your father?
19. What about your mother? Same question.
20. If you were your mother, how would you have raised yourself differently?
21. If you were your father, how would you have raised yourself differently?

This part of the discussion questions has to do with your relationship with each other and the children in your lives.

1. How is your relationship to your mate similar to that of your mother and father?
2. How is it different?
3. How do you show affection for each other?
4. How do you argue or fight?
5. When your children (or stepchildren) are your age, would you want your relationship with them to be similar to the relationship you have with your own parents? If not, how would you like it to be different?
6. Do you have any specific expectations or goals in mind for each of your children (stepchildren)? If so, what are those expectations?

7. Over the next one year, how would you like to change your relationship with one or more of your children (stepchildren)?

8. What are the three most important things of a positive nature your children (stepchildren) can learn from you?

9. What are the three most important things of a negative nature your children (stepchildren) can learn from you?

10. Based on the information you have about each other, are there some significant or minor changes in your relationship which seem to be in order? If so, how should you go about effecting those changes?

11. Are there changes in order between you and your mate? How should you go about making such changes?

Once you have identified and accepted your own values regarding family as a concept, there is an even tougher job ahead. That is to accept the idea that you are not, repeat, not, involved in a family in the sense you have usually understood it.

This means that you, as a stepparent, must search for answers on your own, usually by painful trial and error. It means that you may have to abandon attitudes and values toward the concept of family and family roles that you have cherished from your earliest days. Your position in the family is not traditional, and attempts to establish traditional relationships will not work for you. Instead, you may need to develop a new set of attitudes and values toward the family. Your success hinges on one crucial point: your ability to form your own separate relationship with the children.

The Crucial Point

Let me state this crucial point fully, so that it will remain clear in your mind as you read: You cannot now and probably can never share fully in the relationship between your spouse and his or her children. You can, however, develop a separate relationship with the children that has its own power and satisfaction. The distinction between the two relationships is critical. Your effort to join the first relationship as an equal member is doomed to failure. Your effort to develop your own relationship has a good chance of success, and there is where I suggest you concentrate your efforts.

To establish this important, separate relationship between you and the children requires stamina, self-control, and understanding. It is not easy, but your chances of success are good if you are able to adjust your attitudes toward the family to accurately reflect your function as a stepparent.

Chapter 2

ONLY A PARENT COULD LOVE A KID LIKE THAT

What is Family Bonding?

Whatever their role configuration, whatever their purpose, whatever the relationships are like among their members, families are held together mainly by virtue of an ineluctable force called bonding. Stepparents are rarely joined into the family by this kind of bonding; they remain outside the inner circle where it has sway.

Bonding is a genetic and psychic connection between blood members of families. Its properties elude description. Like air, it cannot be seen directly, but its effects are undeniable. It ebbs and flows through the lives of blood family members, never ceasing to exert influence in mysterious but compelling ways. It is a kind of primal connection between people: a deep awareness of the responsibility toward each other.

The Family Tie

Bonding is the "glue" which holds blood family members together as a distinct social group. It does not depend for its presence upon love or good feelings of any kind; indeed, natural family members may have adverse feelings toward each other. Its main effect is that it commands the attention of one natural family member to another, whatever the thought or attitude that may accompany that attention.

Love and affection between family members may strengthen bonding, but discord and ill will do not diminish it. The concepts of Father, Mother, Child, Brother, and Sister hold special meaning among human beings. Bonding is an irrevocable force, permeating the human spirit to its most subtle depths.

The Tie That Keeps Apart

Bonding is also an exclusionary force. While it holds blood family members in its thrall, it builds impermeable boundaries against intrusion of anyone from outside its domain. It does permit, however, friendships with outsiders. It also permits other bondings to form, such as through marriage and adoption, but they will be new and separate bonding systems, having all the properties of the first. Bonds can run parallel to one another, but they will not blend.

Bonding And Behavior

As strong a force as bonding is, it does not necessarily dictate behavior or attitudes between bonded people. Behavior and attitude are matters of choice for individuals. A divorced man and woman may despise one another, but that strength of feeling only confirms their emotional connection to one another. The same may hold true for the child and parent, or the brother and sister. Real indifference is almost impossible in bonded relationships. Positive feelings have the same character; they can exist beyond any rational explanation, because of the power of bonding.

Thus, bonding transcends the apparent realities to motivate family members to continue, for their lifetime, interaction between themselves. Even if that interaction is only the spirit, without manifestation in behavior, it is there, and it can be felt.

The Human Need for Bonding

Human beings need this bonding force in their lives. It gives a sense of belonging without which life has little or no meaning. Beyond food and shelter, our greatest need is to love and be loved. And bonding provides the spiritual milieu in which love can flourish. It allows tempers and feelings to fluctuate wildly between two people, without threatening the essential, basic trust within the relationship.

Bonding provides humans with a sense of unity and flow. It is like the ocean, seemingly separated by masses of land into smaller seas, but, on a grander scale, forming an ultimate oneness. It is like the river: it may carry sweet water or foul, but it flows, inexorably.

The Fear Of Unbonding

Although bonding does not show itself in attitudes and behavior, it usually has the effect of strongly suggesting them. An example arises from the almost paralyzing fear felt by a natural parent contemplating the loss of bonding with a natural child. This loss can't happen, but the parent and child may not know it. Therefore, out of fear, the parent (or child) may attempt to confirm the existence of bonding with effusive shows of love, respect, obedience, and the like.

Fear of the loss of bonding would be short-lived if there were some method to check for its presence. But bonding has a pervasive quality that cannot be directly perceived, or even inferred, from behavior, attitudes, and language. Bonding can only be felt and understood on the level of instinct. Therefore, the natural parent often persists in mistaking the alleged characteristics of bonding—such as affection, respect, and obedience—for the real thing.

Thus we find a natural mother in panic at hearing her child report a genuine liking for a stepmother or girlfriend of the natural father. A cold fear runs through her at the idea that her bond with her child is being eroded. We find a natural father allowing his visiting children to behave atrociously, because he fears proper discipline will jeopardize his bond with them. We find a child driving emotional wedges between his natural parent and his stepparent, vaguely, sometimes explicitly, working to reunite the pair who provided his first sense of human bonding.

Bonding Between Spouses

Bonding occurs between adults, too. Even a brief marriage is likely to result in the bonding of a man and woman. Regardless of the nature of the relationship, if bonding has occurred, it will stay in place. The dissolution of a marriage may have profound effects on the behavior and attitudes of two people toward each other, but their mutual demand for attention will continue. This is particularly true when children have issued from the marriage. Carl Rogers, the humanistic psychologist, has said that relationships never end, they simply change. He is right. The effects of bonding may diminish over time, but the bond itself remains.

First Spouse First Bond

Second spouses are often exasperated, confused, and hurt by their mate's behavior toward the first spouse. Frequent, apparently unnecessary telephone conversations between first mates cause many second spouses to seriously wonder about their partner's commitment to the second marriage and themselves. Child support and alimony payments, often devastating enough to a second family, sometimes take on what seems an unreasonable priority. First mates sometimes make outrageous demands and have them met, while the second spouse knows full well that his or her own similar demand would be ignored.

If some second spouses have the uncomfortable feeling that their mates are not totally committed to them, they are often correct. People bonded in previous relationships will stay that way. It is part of the condition of being human, a valuable condition, albeit a sometimes difficult one to accept in one's own spouse.

The Odd Man Out

Even if you have a clear, unambiguous understanding of your beliefs in the purpose and nature of Family, you must adjust to the lack of bonding in your relationship with your stepchildren. No natural, instinctual force pulls you and the children together in a mutually satisfying way. Often, an instinctual force pushes you apart. Whereas natural parents rely on the underlying bond to preserve their relationship to their children, you must rely only upon observed behavior and emotional tone between you and your stepchildren.

If you try to assume the role of a mother or father, you will almost inevitably be disappointed. The satisfaction in those callings derive from family bonding, not from the simple assumption of roles. So it is for children who delightedly enter a step-relationship, only to be disappointed when natural bonding does not occur. Their satisfaction as children comes from the bonding to a natural parent, not from the role of child itself.

The exclusionary effects of bonding on stepparents need not be a cause for despair. You are a person, and so is your stepchild. Bonding between two persons is always possible if they are open to its formation. It is important to understand, however, that when bonding occurs between you and your stepchildren, it is likely to be a separate bond from that between the children and their natural parents. This separate relationship can be delightful, rewarding, and as equally powerful as any other. But it is the wise stepparent who, having achieved such a relationship, leaves well enough alone and tries not to intrude upon other bonded systems.

Relationships By Choice

We seek relationships for a variety of reasons. Chief among them is our need to love and be loved. Specifically, we put effort into relationships that make us feel good about ourselves and others. When we meet people with whom we can't achieve those results, we normally avoid a relationship and seek out others. Ultimately, we are engaged in a lifelong search for bondings with as many others as we can find.

For a relationship to continue, some initial conditions must be met. Each individual has a need of being dealt with as he thinks he deserves. A stranger who refuses your offer of a handshake is not likely to be pursued. A snarl in response to a smile does not encourage closeness.

Most meetings between you and other people

are chance occurrences, and you always have the choice to accept or reject the companionship. If, by happy chance, you find your needs being met at least superficially by the association with another, you may choose to explore the relationship to see how far it may go. This choice, which is usually exercised early in relationships, is based primarily on how you expect to be treated.

The No-Choice Relationship

Stepparents and stepchildren have a different type of relationship. They have no choice but to associate with one another for what is expected to be a lifetime. People of vastly different ages, personalities, and interests arbitrarily join lives. Would you have chosen your stepchild as a lifelong companion?

Stepparents and stepchildren often resent not only this lack of freedom to choose their companion, but also the lack of freedom to discontinue the relationship. Interaction is forced upon them, for good or ill.

Forcing Matters

An enforced interaction often takes on a direction of its own. For example, stepparents often feel that they overreact to routine situations. In an effort to end an annoying situation, their reactions and demands may become unreasonably harsh. The forcefulness of such reactions has the tendency to accelerate the development of whole patterns of negative behavior between children and stepparents. If these patterns are accepted as evidence of the overall tone of a relationship, they can lead to profound misunderstandings and undermine subsequent efforts for better relations.

Toward A More Natural Relationship

Because you and your stepchildren are not bonded, and because your mutual involvement is arbitrairly imposed upon you, the basic conditions for mutually satisfying relationships could well be missing. In this case, the keystone for your success as a stepparent is your ability to permit yourself not to love or to be loved by your stepchildren. Your stepchildren's entrance into your life is incidental to your relationship with your mate.

There is no natural reason for you and the children to love each other, and there are usually some good reasons not to. The focus of your relationship should be on how you interact, rather than on what motivates your interaction. The way you behave toward each other will define the positive or negative value of your relationship. With that principle in mind, you are free to structure your relationships with your stepchildren in such a way that bonding is neither demanded nor expected.

Essentially, you and your spouse need to set up a mutually agreeable structure of family relationships in which you, as an unbonded member, have at least the opportunity to find value in your interaction with the children. The structure needs to be flexible, but sturdy enough to bear repeated internal misunderstandings, dislike, and downright attempts to sabotage the structure.

A mutually beneficial structure is not easy to construct and is even harder to keep standing. It is often as arbitrary and contrived a structure as the pattern of relationship it is replacing. Nevertheless, it represents an honest, carefully thought out consideration of the realities of the situation. At worst, it establishes the behavioral and attitudinal conditions under which you and the children can operate with the least amount of friction. At best, it offers a framework for all family members to work toward a honest, forthright relationship with each other.

More of this in the next chapter.

Chapter 3

FORGING A NEW FAMILY STRUCTURE

The structure of family relationships you set up should depend primarily on your understanding of how you need to be treated and how you define your responsibilities toward your stepchildren. How you would see yourself if you were a natural parent does not enter the picture. When you take into account your unbonded status with the children, you will recognize the limits of your responsibility toward them and your parent partner.

Who's Responsible for The Kids?

You are not responsible, unless you choose to be, for the formation of a child's character. A child's character may be affected by your character and personality over time, but you have no natural responsiblity over how a child develops. That is the natural parent's job. To an extent, the child is an extension of the parent, and it is the parent's prerogative to define the direction, form, and behavior of that extension.

A natural parent has made a choice, by having children, to subjugate some of his or her own needs to the needs of the child. This choice is inherent in the decision to have children. Whether the natural parent understood this at the time of the child's conception is irrelevant, as is the matter of whether the natural parent now values or regrets the choice. The essential responsibility for the development of a child remains with the natural parents despite divorce and remarriage.

Taking Responsibility Is a Decision

Any effort you make to assume or share parental responsibility should derive from a clear, explicit decision to do so. In addition, the decision should be made explicit to your partner, with discussion of what the decision entails regarding your acceptance of roles and duties.

Remember, however, that your primary responsibility is to yourself. Any commitments you make with respect to stepchildren should be made with your own best interests in mind. This statement is not a prescription for irresponsible selfishness, nor is it a call for child neglect. It is a recognition that any relationship you commit yourself to by choice must be self-satisfying, or the relationship will ultimately be no good for anyone concerned. Your marriage represents a judgment about how best to meet your own needs, so let your judgment about how to be involved with the children have the same motivation.

When Old Assumptions Lead Astray: *An Example*

Before taking on responsibilities, it is important to carefully check all your assumptions. Check your assumptions. All your feelings and behavior are based on old assumptions about your proper place in the scheme of things. My experience is that stepparents having trouble are usually acting upon assumptions which, when made explicit, do not accurately represent their needs.

The following dialogue with a stepmother will help illustrate the blinding power of old assumptions. To this stepmother, the problems she was having with her husband had one cause: he would not accept her comments on his children without getting his feelings hurt. I'll call her Joan and her husband Paul

Joan   "Paul and I get in some terrible fights when I even suggest one of the children is not perfect. I feel so frustrated when I tell him what one of them is doing, and he just tries to make me feel guilty."

Pete   "Why do you report these observations of yours to Paul?"

Joan   "Well, I think he ought to know about the things they are doing. He'll just sit there and watch them do the most outrageous things and never lift a finger. If they misbehave while he's gone and I tell him about it, he acts like I'm making it up and gets mad at me for telling him. It's gotten so I can't handle them, and he won't."

Pete   "I see. Does Paul expect you to handle them?"

Joan.   "Well, somebody has to."

Pete.   "Why?"

Joan.   "Those kids are going to grow up thinking they can get away with anything. They won't have respect for anyone or anything. I'm really worried about them."

Pete. "Back to Paul for a moment. Does Paul expect you to teach them this respect?"

Joan. "I don't really know. He sure gets mad when I try to do anything about them."

Pete. "Perhaps that tells you something."

Joan. "I can't believe Paul wants his kids to grow up the way they are going. I sure wouldn't if they were my children."

Pete. "Let me check some assumptions with you, Joan, and see if we can get to the heart of your frustration. You assume Paul does not understand his children to be lacking in respect, or that they ever misbehave."

Joan. "Let me see. No, that's not quite right. He's not blind or stupid. He can see how they behave sometimes, he just won't do anything about it."

Pete. "Okay. Then you assume if you reinforce his awareness that they misbehave, he will change his attitude and cause them to act differently."

Joan. "I guess I have been assuming that, but I've been at it for two years now, and it hasn't **gotten** me anywhere."

Pete. "Are you sure you and Paul have the same definition of what misbehavior is?"

Joan. "Now that you mention it, I'm not so sure we do. When he doesn't get downright mad at me, he usually tells me I'm making a mountain out of a molehill. I've always thought that was because he just refuses to discuss their behavior. He really confused me one time when I told him the nine year old had gone to the store without permission and he said, "Good." When I asked him what he meant, he said he was glad the kid was developing some independence. I couldn't tell whether he was serious or not, so I just let it drop."

Pete. "Uh huh. Joan, have you ever directly asked Paul whether or not he wants you to influence his thinking about the children?

Joan. "Well, not directly. I mean, not point-blank just like that. I am his wife, after all, and I have to deal with the children, too."

Pete. "Yes, of course you do. By being his wife, I take it you mean you believe you and Paul should share the same attitudes about the children, and that he would naturally want your input about them."

Joan. "Yes, something like that."

Pete. "A moment ago you said you wouldn't want the children to grow up the way they were going, if they were yours."

Joan. "That's for sure."

Pete. "Okay. That means you do not share Paul's view of how children should be handled."

Joan. "Right."

Pete. "And you assume your views are better than Paul's."

Joan. "Well, that's kind of a blunt way to put it, but, yes, I do."

Pete. "For whom?"

Joan. "I'm getting confused. You're trying to get me to say I don't have the right to help Paul with the children, and I shouldn't expect them to behave."

Pete. "On the contrary. I'm inviting you to examine what "help" means, according to Paul. It's already clear you and Paul have different ideas about what good behavior means. Your expectations are different from Paul's. If you and Paul wish to avoid your unhappy conflicts about the children, one of you is going to have to change your expectations to match with the other's, or you're both going to have to openly accept the fact you have different expectations and work from there. In effect, it seems you have been trying to get Paul to, as you say, help you with the children, by adopting your expectations. That hasn't worked because you define the meaning of their behavior in different ways. What is misbehavior to you, is a show of independence to Paul, for instance. You are working at cross purposes. Let me see if I can identify the assumption you've been working upon, and see if it really fits with what you want to do. You have assumed you should take on the role of a natural mother, thus taking responsibility for breeding into the children certain personality traits you would wish your own children to have. Right?"

Joan. "Yes. But I don't really want to be their mother. They already have one, and I think three parents are too many for any kid."

Pete. "Okay. Then you may assume you are not responsible for how the children turn out, the responsibility of that being Paul's and his former wife's."

Joan. "If you put it that way, yes."

Pete. "Does that feel better for you?"

Joan. "It sure does. I'm feeling better already, like a load is being lifted off my shoulders. But what about my fights with Paul?"

Pete. "Based on your now assumption of your role, are any fights necessary?"

Joan. "Why no, I guess not. If he is ultimately responsible for them, I can just let him use his own best judgment about how to handle them. Why should I beat my brains out trying to get him to agree with me? It would be different if we had children together though, wouldn't it?"

Pete. "Sure. But let's take one thing at a time. You still have the problem of getting the children to behave in an acceptable way for you."

Joan. "Yeah. Well, when I'm with them alone, they do pretty well. They mind all right, and I even enjoy them some of the time. The problems start when we're all together."

Pete. "I see. So the children already know you and Paul have different expectations and act accordingly when Paul is around."

Joan. "Yes, it's like they're different kids altogether."

Pete. "What would happen if you suggested to Paul that any time he is with the children, he is to be completely in charge, but that he should first discuss with you any decision about the children when they are to be alone with you?"

Joan. "To tell the truth, I think he'd like that. He doesn't like these fights any better than I do. But I think the kids would go hog wild and drive us nuts."

Pete. "You think that if Paul is in complete charge, he would allow himself and you to go nuts."

Joan. "Well, no. Not really. I guess if we weren't spending most of our energy on a battle to see who's going to get control, he would

45

handle things all right. I might not like some of his decisions, but maybe it would be good for him. I guess I've been trying to take some of his responsibilities away from him. If he agrees to this, should we tell the kids what we're doing?"

Pete. "Sure. You can bet they have been as confused as you and Paul have been, caught in the middle of this struggle for control. As the authority changes hands from time to time, you might just tell the kids simply, "Your dad is in charge, ask him," or "Joan is in charge, ask her." Then stick to it."

Joan. "That's going to be the key, isn't it? Sticking to it."

Pete. "Yes."

An Analysis

The foregoing dialogue is representative of hundreds of conversations with stepparents and their partners. Joan's problems stemmed mainly from her assumption that she had a duty to direct the lives of Paul and his children. When she tried to perform her supposed duty, she ran into resistance from Paul. Paul, apparently, did not share her assumption that she was to direct his life with his children. The result was confused anger in both of them.

Joan and Paul agreed to try separating their roles, and it has worked out well. Joan no longer feels that Paul must handle his children her way, and Paul is no longer caught in the dilemma of trying to match his wife's values and trying to raise his children by his own, different values. Since this episode, he has taken on more responsibility for the kids, and Joan has noticed (with a kind of smug glee) that his behavior toward the children is now more closely attuned to hers. She is clever enough not to rub it in.

What this couple has done is simple. They changed the structure and pattern of their relationship so that each could deal more effectively with the children in his own way. They set clear boundaries for each partner's respective responsibilities.

Mutuality Between Natural Parents

When both natural parents are present in a family, the parents generally have mutually understood, consistent expectations for the children. These consistent expectations develop through a long series of mutually supportive interactions during the years of pregnancy, infancy, and childhood. Both persons have experienced an uninterrupted exchange of ideas and attitudes that facilitates understanding, if not agreement, between them. As a result, their values and expectations are generally consistent.

From this history of adaptation and understanding, natural parents acquire perceptions of their roles and responsibilities as parents. These perceptions are formed piecemeal, with small but important shifts and adaptations over time. These perceptions adjust, augment, or reinforce earlier role concepts tracing back to experiences in each person's own family of origin.

The result is consistency of purpose and understanding. In addition, the natural parents have the historical foundations for further adaptation and greater ability to understand shifts in attitudes between them. Doubtlessly, consistency of purpose and mutually agreed upon goals can make good parenting easier.

Mutuality Between Natural Parents and Stepparents

If mutuality is achieved between a natural parent and a stepparent, so much the better, but it is rare, mainly because the stepparent does not share a history of adaptation with the natural parent and the children. Whatever your ideas may be concerning child raising, you will likely find them clashing with your spouse's firmly established system of beliefs, forged through thousands of both explicit and subtle interactions with someone else.

I do not mean to say that all natural parents agree with each other about the way to raise their children, for of course they do not. Your partner may have views entirely opposite from the views of his or her former spouse. Even so, your partner's beliefs are rooted deeply in experience that you cannot share and that you cannot change.

The conventional wisdom offered for good parenting is that there should be no separation of roles, that is, boundaries, between parents with respect to dealing with children, that children should be able to deal with both parents as if the parents were of one mind, that the expectations of one parent should be the expectations of the other. This principal has become almost an article of faith among adults dealing with children.

Between stepparents and natural parents, however, such consistency of purpose and expectations is often impossible. No matter how hard you try, you may find yourself unable to appreciate or condone your partner's style of thinking and behaving toward the children, let alone adopt your partner's views.

When this is the case, you may find yourself trying desperately to get your partner to adopt your beliefs about effective parenting. Our friend

49

Joan discovered the futility of that approach. On the other hand, you may find yourself subordinating your beliefs to those of your spouse. This approach fails also. Without total conviction and understanding of your spouse's methods, you cannot effectively support his or her efforts consistently. Instead, you are likely to undermine and be undermined all along the way.

Establishing Boundaries

Only clear, consistent, predictable kinds of relationships are able to grow. This does not mean that children will suffer if the adults do not share the same goals and purposes for them. Your expectations about the behavior of children should be self-consistent, but not necessarily consistent with those of your spouse. All that is really necessary is that everyone understand your particular expectations. You can, and should, draw clear and explicit boundaries between you and your mate. There is no point in pretending you and your partner have mutual goals and needs with respect to the children if, indeed, you do not. The children will only become confused or very adept at playing you and your partner against each other.

For example, if you and your partner do not agree about the efficacy of spanking children for misbehavior, agree to disagree. Explain to the children you will deal with them in one way, and your partner will deal with them in another. All that is really necessary is that you and your partner do not enterfere with each other's handling of things. As long as you, your partner, and the children understand what your expectations and needs are, and you insist on them, that is all the consistency required.

The idea is to establish and maintain a structure within which you can work, not to try to fit yourself into a structure of interactions with which you cannot be comfortable. Between you and your mate, there needs to be a high level of cooperation, but not necessarily agreement. The cooperation should take the form of a mutual willingness to develop and maintain the kind of relationship with the children that works best for each of you individually. Where patterns of relationship are similar, cooperation between you and your partner will be naturally easy; where they are dissimilar, cooperation becomes difficult, but absolutely essential.

Remember, as you develop workable patterns of responsibility in your family, that your main goal is to enhance the quality of your own life. You are not morally or legally bound to live out your life in an altruistc abandonment of your own needs for the needs of those around you. If you take care of yourself, you will, in the long run, take better care of those you are involved with.

The Importance of Being Direct

For relationships to be effective, they need to be direct. Directness means straightforward dealing with others, whether children or spouse. You allow no one else to convey your needs or to act as an intermediary between you and another person. If you want something done, do it yourself. If you want someone to do something, tell them yourself what you want done, and how, and when. If you want to do something for someone else, make sure they understand the intended spirit behind what you do, and be sure it is something they really want done for them.

The most common form of indirect dealings is the stepparent's communicating to the child through the natural parent. You may be finding yourself asking your mate to tell the children to take out the garbage, to clean up their room, or to be home on time from school. If you need the children to do things for you, ask them directly, only making sure you have the authority from the natural parent.

The Indirect Approach . . .

A man of my acquaintance had the family task of dropping his teenage stepson off at a school on the way to his office. The morning routine in their household was for the mother to get the boy up early enough so that he would be ready to go when his stepfather was leaving. For his own reasons, the boy would stall and procrastinate, forcing the stepfather to be late for work several mornings a week. His mother would plead, threaten, and cajole each morning, and the boy would acquiesce or curse, depending on his mood. It was becoming a painful experience for everyone. The stepfather left without him a few times in an attempt to motivate the boy. That tactic only resulted in afterschool detention for the boy and the disruption of family life in the evening.

After several months of the mother's unsuccessful efforts with the boy, the stepfather examined the pattern of the morning routine and came to the conclusion that he was the only one who was not getting his needs met. He had to get to work on time, and the boy was holding him up.

. . . Versus the Direct Approach

The stepfather announced to his wife that she was no longer in charge of rousing the boy in the morning, that he would assume the task himself. She reluctantly agreed, knowing there was trouble ahead. The boy and his stepfather didn't have a very good relationship to begin with, and she knew how cantankerous her son was in the morning. Both of them announced to the son that his stepfather would be getting him up in the morning from now on. The boy snickered.

For the first few days, the stepfather copied his wife's methods. He pleaded, threatened, and cajoled, as she had been doing, with about the same lack of success. Still, the boy needed to get to school, and the stepdad needed to get to work. Still, every day started off in anger and verbal abuse. The mother was afraid, with good reason, that there might be physical blows some morning.

Finally, in desperation, the stepfather decided he had had enough. On a Wednesday evening he showed the boy the squirt gun he had purchased that day. He explained he would henceforth engage in no morning arguments. He would, he said, gently ask the boy, once, to get up. There after, at two minute intervals, he would squirt the boy with ice water. It would be the boy's choice to raise himself or not. The boy responded by saying he would punch the stepfather out if he did that. The stepfather retorted that at least the boy would have to get up to try.

Thursday morning, the stepfather asked the boy, gently, to get up. The boy replied with the usual curses and remained in bed. Two minutes later, the stepfather stood in the boy's doorway and squirted him with ice water. The boy bounded out of bed in a rage, screaming obscenities. The stepfather simply turned and walked away. In spite of the threats, the boy did not attack him. The ride to school was unpleasant, but both were on time. The next morning, the stepfather repeated the routine, only this time the boy continued to stay in bed for a second, then a third squirting. When the fourth squirting time came around, the boy was already in the shower. The third morning the boy got up at the first request, sullen, but up.

For the next few weeks, the squirt gun was used only a few times, and eventually it did not have to be used at all. The stepfather stood by his promise not to engage in any arguments in the morning. After about a month, both the boy and the stepfather found themselves looking forward to sharing their morning coffee in the car together. Their relationship began to change radically for the better.

In this true story, the stepfather rearranged his relationship with the stepson from an indirect to a direct one. He had a need, and until he directly stated and pursued his own goal, his need could not be met. He had depended on the efforts of his wife to get something done that only he could do.

What You Will Accept Is Not Always What You Want

A second crucial factor in the story's outcome was that the stepfather discovered the difference between what he wanted and what he would accept in the boy's behavior. In his heart, the stepfather would have preferred cooperation and love. Without these, the stepfather accepted something attainable, namely, an amicable enough relationship with the boy to allow him to get to work on time. Having clearly identified his own, practical need, he worked until he had met it. He set clear boundaries between himself and his stepson. With those firmly in place, both began to understand their relationship could be released from its bitter deadlock and moved in positive directions.

When specific behavioral expectations are made explicit, you and your stepchildren have an opportunity to work toward better feelings about yourselves and each other. But your expectations must be within the realm of possibilities for your relationship to succeed. This requires that you make a clear differentiation between what you want and can't have and what you will accept and can have.

The Double Bind

In a recent seminar, a man aired his frustration in getting his three stepchildren to show responsibility in doing household chores. The problem was not that the children refused to perform assigned tasks; rather, the children never showed enough self-motivation to suit the father. This lack on initiative disappointed the father, for he wanted his children to share his own high sense of responsibility. Thus, if the children did the tasks, he was unhappy because he felt the children acted upon their desire to please him and not upon their own sense of family responsibility. Of course, if the tasks were not done, he was unhappy because this would be further proof that the children had little sense of responsibility. As a result, the children could not please their stepfather whether they did what he asked or not.

This is what is known as the double bind. The theory for it comes from Gregory Bateson who tried to determine how people become schizophrenic. Briefly, a double bind results from expectations that cannot possibly be met, even by people who have a genuine interest in satisfying each other's needs. For example, if I ask you to spontaneously stand up, and you wish to satisfy my request, what will you do? If you stand up, I will be disappointed because you have not done it spontaneously; I had to ask you to do it. If you lie down spontaneously, I will be disappointed because you did not stand up. You cannot have the satisfaction of meeting my expectation, nor can I have the satisfaction of your having met it. All this because I have made not one, but two requests that cancel each other out. Both of us are immobilized and we will be dissatisfied by that immobilization as well. Nobody can do anything right.

This is what was happening with the man at the seminar. He wanted the children to do household chores, but he wanted them to do the chores voluntarily. So, he was disappointed in them. The fact they would do the chores at his request was irrelevant; his satisfaction in the successful completion of the chores was canceled out by his dissatisfaction with the quality of their motivation. Because the children could not share his sense of responsibility, they could only disappoint him.

The Double Bind in Marriages

This sort of thing happens frequently between married couples, particularly around sexual needs. There is often an expectation that the partner will know what to do and how to do it. I can't count the times I have heard people say things like, "If she/he really loved me, she/he would know what I want and do it." An accurate rephrasing of that statement is, "I have concluded my partner does not love me because I know my partner has the magical ability to read my mind and is therefore deliberately ignoring my sexual needs. Moreover, if my partner cannot magically read my mind, then she/he does not love me, or else is deficient and not worthy of me."

This kind of thinking combines an expectation that cannot be met with one that can. No one can read minds, but almost everyone can perform sexually. If you allow the fact that you have to tell your partner how to satisfy you to diminish your sexual pleasure, you have set up a double bind whereby neither of you can ever be sexually satisfied. Both of you will be far better off if you will accept what is possible, sexual pleasure, and abandon the expectation for the impossible, mind reading.

Avoiding The Double Bind

Whenever you develop an expectation for a stepchild, make sure it is one that the child can meet and one that both of you can observe objectively. For instance, do not expect a child to love you; the child may not be able to do that. But you can expect a child to use a respectful tone of voice and civilized language when dealing with you. By the same token, do not expect yourself to love the stepchild; you may not be able to do that. But you can expect yourself to treat the child in a civilized manner.

If you notice that both of you are succeeding in the possible expectations you have set, you may genuinely congratulate yourselves and feel good about each other. That mutuality of met expectations may become the basis for a more fulfilling relationship.

Restructuring: *A cooperative Effort*

Structuring a direct relationship with your stepchildren requires the cooperation of your partner, of course, no matter how you choose to structure things. Getting this cooperation may require changes in your relationship with your partner as well.

To restructure a relationship wisely requires that both adults reveal their expectations of each other. Your partner undoubtedly has certain expectations of you as a stepparent, whether they have been made explicit or not. You certainly have some expectations of yourself as a stepparent, explicit or not. Thus, the first step toward a cooperative relationship with your partner is to get clear statements from each other about what those expectations are. If you have not already done this in a formal way, do it. If it helps to write it down, do that.

First, identify what you want. What would be the optimal situation for each of you? If you both could wave a magic wand and have things perfect for each of you, what would those things be? Do this separately, so that both of you can make clear statements of your needs without the influence of the other's presence.

You will probably be reluctant to state what you really want and how you really feel, or reluctant to share the information with your spouse. You will not like some of the things you want and need, and you will be sure your partner won't like them either. List them anyway, and insist on your partner being as honest and thorough as you. Count on the fact that, while both of you will probably get your feelings hurt, you nevertheless will develop a basis for better cooperation in the future.

The format for this exercise should be a series of sentences beginning with "I want . . ." and "I need . . ." One stepmother's list began this way:

"I want a loving, exciting marriage with my husband."

"I want his children completely out of our lives."

"If I can't have that, I need him to tell me the

absolute minimum I must do with his children in order to satisfy him."

Her husband's list began this way:

"I want my wife to be a mother for my children."

"I want her to love them and for them to love her."

"I want her to have charge of all domestic matters and to enjoy it."

The lists went further, but you can see they began with radically opposite ideas. I hope yours are not quite so polarized. Even if they are, however, you can begin to structure your relationship in a manner that will work for both of you. This is the aim of the next part of the exercise.

Exchange your lists of wants and needs. Agree beforehand you will not argue or fight with each other when you do. There are likely to be some surprises for both of you, some pleasant, some not so pleasant. The most common statement I hear from folks when they do this is "I didn't know that's the way you really feel." Remember, these statements are honest expressions of your deeply felt needs and are to be respected as such. Each of you has risked a great deal to present them to your partner, and neither of you is to judge or be judged in the process of being honest.

Now give yourselves a day or two to examine

each other's statements. Take the time to get over your hurt (if you're hurt) and prepare for the next step.

The next step is to determine what you will accept in behavior from the other. This is important. State clearly what you will accept in the way of behavior. This does not mean that either of you is giving up what you want; it means only that you state what you will accept in behavior if you can't get what you want. You are in the process of avoiding the trap of double binding each other.

The stepmother came back with the following, for example:

"I want a loving, exciting marriage with my husband, and I will accept nothing less. I will devote at least one hour a day to thinking up and implementing things I know will please him. I expect him to do the same."

"I will accept responsibility for all the family laundry and meal preparation. I will perform biweekly major housecleaning, but I expect my husband to be responsible, by himself or with the children, for daily house and kitchen cleaning chores. I will not necessarily enjoy the tasks I set forth, but I will do them."

"When I must deal with the children on my own, I expect to have complete authority from my husband to handle them the best way I know how, without interference. I will accept the responsibility of being as supportive of them as I can be, but I will not promise to love them any more than they can promise to love me. I only hope that will come."

The husband's list began with the following:

"I will accept from my wife a promise to do her best to keep the level of friction between her and the children to a minimum, but I will not abandon my children for her sake."

"I will accept half, in terms of time, of the domestic duties around the house."

Happiness Is A Bargain

Make no mistake. This is a bargaining process, the object of which is the enhancement of the quality of life for all of you. Make your needs and wants known, decide what you will accept in the way of behavior, then stick to it. You and your partner are clearly differentiating your roles with respect to the children. If you reach some areas where you can't agree, and you probably will, agree to disagree. State what you will or won't do, and hold your ground. Expect your partner to do the same. The anger and resentment you may feel toward one another now is small payment for the elimination of differences and misunderstandings that can plague a lifetime. Only in this manner can you achieve a set of realistic expectations of each other and achieve a pattern of behavior in which you can feel good about yourself and your partner. A trust and understanding develop within the behavioral boundaries you each have set, other variations become possible.

Summary

Since you do not have the advantage of bonding with the children, base your relationship with them on acceptable behavior. Have clear boundaries drawn with respect to responsibility and authority. Develop your expectations from what is possible to achieve and observe. Be particularly alert to avoid involving yourself, your mate, and the children in destructive double binds.

Through clear, thorough negotiations with your spouse, establish a structure of relationships in your household whereby you can have your own needs met, whatever they are. Make sure that your spouse does not have to guess at your needs to provide for them.

Where the children are concerned, do the same. Make your needs and expectations clear, then insist they deal directly with you when there is a conflict. Do not interact with your stepchildren through your spouse. If the children are old enough, ask them to clarify what they expect from you, and negotiate your needs with them.

The most important thing is to create clear lines of communication and responsibility. Rely only upon yourself to get your needs met.

Chapter 4

FINDING THE RIGHT WORDS

As you go about the business of improving interaction within your family, you may need to spiff up your own style of communication. There are hundreds of books on effective communication, some of which will help you improve your ability to communicate well. In stepparented families, however, certain problems seem to arise more frequently than in other types of households. These problems we will discuss in this chapter.

Keep in mind, as you read, two self-evident facts about personal communications. The first is: All verbal and nonverbal behavior communicates something. It is impossible for two people who have even slight contact with each other not to communicate on some level. The second is: Communication is effective only to the degree it conveys the intended meaning.

"We Can't Communicate"

Couples come to me and say, "We have a problem. We don't communicate." I agree with them, they have a problem, but I still don't know what that problem is. They have confused me. I know it is impossible not to communicate, so I must clarify the problem with them or begin making some assumptions about the nature of their problem. The assumptions I would make are either that they find themselves ineffective at communicating with each other, or that they communicate very effectively and don't like what they see and hear.

But one of the principles of good communication is never to make assumptions, or at least to check out assumptions for their validity. So I might say to them, "I don't think it's possible not to communicate at all. Do you mean you are having misunderstandings?" Often I get a response like, "Yeah, she knows damn good and well what I want, and I'm getting sick and tired of . . .," etc. Then I know the nature of the problem.

Unintended Communications

When I say noncommunication is impossible, I mean that people around you will ascribe meaning to your every mannerism. If your stepchild walks in the house and you are napping on the couch, the child will assign a meaning to that. The child may simply assume you were tired and fell asleep, or that you are indirectly telling her you have no interest whatsoever in her arrival. The fact of your being there, doing what you're doing, communicates something. You may not have intended a message to the child, but you sent one. This is an example of communication over which you have no control.

But you do have control over most of your communications, if you choose to exercise it. And if you choose to be effective, here are five principles to guide you.

Rule 1: Never Assume

Any time you make an assumption about what a stepchild (or anyone, for that matter) thinks or feels, you run a high risk of being wrong. Any time you are acting upon assumptions, you are acting on what is likely to be poor information.

Ask whatever questions you need in order to make sure both you and the other family member are operating on the same basis of understanding. Phrases like, "Let me make sure I understand you . . .," "I'll repeat what you just told me and you let me know if I've got it straight . . .," "Please repeat what I just said so we both know we understand each other . . .," are helpful.

Trust your own instincts when you feel uneasy about whether you have understood or been understood. Understanding is different from being believed or agreed with, but it is fundamental to working out disagreements and to persuading someone toward a different view.

Differences in Knowledge

Be very careful about assuming knowledge on the part of anyone else, especially children. Children often mask their lack of understanding of words and concepts that adults take for granted.

For example, I had an important function to attend one evening and carefully instructed my five-year-old to be home from play before dark, having him repeat my instructions so that there would be no misunderstanding. When he arrived twenty minutes past sundown and I began to scold him, he looked so confused and hurt that I thought I'd better check it out. He told me, through his tears, that it was not dark and he didn't know why I was mad at him. When I pointed out the window and told him it was dark out there, he said it was not. Dark was when he got up in the morning.

Differences In Vocabulary

It is also wise to be very careful about the vocabulary you use with children. You can get a fair idea of a child's vocabulary range if you look through a few of last year's school books. Any word you use that is not used in school is probably a word the child doesn't understand.

Differences In Emphasis

Children do not place the same emphasis on certain things that you do. Their sense of time, for instance, is likely to be different from yours. Whereas you might attach significance to, say, the 8:00 a.m. work hour, a child may have only a vague awareness of time, but a keen anticipation of the 8:00 school bell. The bell has either rung or it has not, no matter what time it is.

Differences In Conceptual Values

Neither can you safely assume that children share conceptual values with you. Dressing, for instance, is for most younger children an entirely dispensable part of their lives. Your exasperation over the time it takes a young child to dress is probably incomprehensible to the child. Dressing is a thing of little importance to the child. That little thread peeking out from a pants cuff may be a mystery worth exploring, though. An adolescent, too, may not understand your exasperation. To the teenager, being dressed properly (by his definition), no matter how long it takes, may be the most important thing in the world.

For younger children, concepts of size, space, and shape are different from yours. Big and little, far and near, long and short, up and down, round and square—all are concepts on which you and your children may have entirely different views.

In treating an eight-year-old, for example, I got involved in a guessing game about animals. I was to guess what was big, and round, lived in a cave, and couldn't be hurt. "Ah," I thought, "a protected species of large animal with a basically round shape." The cave threw me a little, but maybe that was a fiction of the child's.

"Elephant?" I said.

"Nope."

"Hippopotamus?"

"No, silly."

"Bear?"

"Uh uh."

"I give up."

"It's an armadillo. What else?"

I know a six-year-old who rode a fly to see her grandma. (Fly = Airplane.) And there is a twelve-year-old who already knows the wind is caused by trees waving back and forth like big fans, but he wants to know what makes the trees start moving.

In summary, never make assumptions unless you have such good information beforehand that you can trust them. Check things out when you feel uneasy. Equally important, make sure whomever you're dealing with is not making false assumptions about you, your motives, or your understanding.

Rule 2: Think first. Know Precisely What You Want To Convey

Many communications go awry because the communicator doesn't really know what he is trying to convey, or for some reason, is unwilling to convey what he means.

When your stepdaughter leaves your makeup scattered all over the bathroom, you have a wide range of emotional responses. They are likely to come in a rush of mixed feelings and intentions. Your effectiveness in dealing with both the mess and your stepchild depends on how you sort out the messages you want to send to the child.

Emotional Versus Reasoned Responses

I was at the home of some friends when this very situation came up. The twelve-year-old stepdaughter was playing a board game in the down stairs den with her brother. Suddenly her stepmother came storming down the stairs and angrily said to the girl, "You are the most irresponsible child I have ever seen. Go to your room and don't come out until I tell you to." The girl had been playing with her stepmother's makeup hours before, had left quite a mess, and my friend had just found it. Having dispatched the girl to her room, the stepmother proceeded to clean up the mess, fuming all the while. After forty-five minutes or so, the stepmother called to the girl, still in an angry tone, "You can come out of your room now, but don't you ever do that again."

I kept quiet, but I couldn't help thinking my friend had not accomplished her real purpose. Later, alone with the little girl, I asked what had made her stepmom so mad (although I already knew). She shrugged her shoulders and said, "I guess she thought I was cheating or something, but I wasn't. I wish she didn't think I was so 'bad."

Here is approximately what the stepmother had conveyed to this child, although not in so many words.

I am angry at you.

I believe you are the worst child in existence.

I believe you cheat at board games with your brother.

I make false judgments about what you do.

I punish you for things you have not done.

I quietly clean up messes you leave without telling you about them.

You may use my makeup whenever you wish and leave a mess, because you may assume it's all right since I have not mentioned it.

Obviously, these were not the messages she intended to send to the girl. Had she stopped to think, she might have called the girl to the bathroom and said,

This is a mess.

I am angry at you for two reasons. You used my makeup without my permission, and you left a mess.

I now expect you to clean up this mess to my satisfaction. If you want to use my makeup in the future, you must ask my permission, and you must clean up any mess you make. When you finish cleaning this up, I expect you to spend a half hour in your room. This is to help you remember to be more responsible in the future.

This is powerful, effective communication. The child sees clearly the stepmother's problem and understands the stepmother's method of solving the problem.

Communicate With A Goal In Mind

Effective communication takes good planning, and planning cannot begin without a clear goal. Any time you rush into an emotional exchange, particularly if you're angry, you increase the likelihood that you will be misunderstood. If your language is ineffective, you won't get your own needs met, and you'll end up getting angrier.

If you want to get an important message across to your listener, then you must take responsibility for the act of communication. If someone is left confused by your words, that's your fault. In addition, it is your responsibility to make sure your listener does not respond to you on false assumptions.

If you need to communicate important ideas to another, whether pleasant or not, ask yourself, "What do I want to accomplish?" If you'll do this habitually, you'll be amazed at how much better people will respond to you. When you know what you want out of an interaction, your verbal and nonverbal language takes on power, precision, and direction.

When You Don't Know What To Say

At times, when you are confused on an issue, you may not know what it is you really want to accomplish. Some issues are too complex to handle hastily. In this case, give yourself time to sort things out. Tell the other person that you don't know what you want right now, but, when you figure it out, you'll come back to the problem. The other person will respect your honesty, if you are frank with them about needing some time.

There are also times when you are unwilling to express your desire. A clear, concise statement such as, "I wish you were dead," may be accurate, but hardly likely to improve the relationship. Your job is to find a specific message that will serve to satisfy at least some of your needs. Something simple like, "I want to be alone for a while," might serve you best.

The mental process required when you can't determine what you want in a particular situation is to shift your attention to some area in which you can obtain a goal. Often, when you can't get a child (or an adult) to do something you need, shift your thinking to something you can do yourself. When you're in a bind, turn the problem back upon yourself. What can *you* do or say to alleviate your frustration with other people's actions or inactions?

Rule 3: Give Information Only About Yourself

Much communication fails because the participants are spending more energy defending themselves against accusations than they are exchanging views. You can curtail almost all argument by restricting the discussion to indisputable information. The only indisputable information that you can offer is information about yourself. No one can deny information you give about yourself, if it is honest.

Taking The Dispute Out Of Disputable

If you say to your mate, "You never help me with the children," you are telling your mate something about him-or herself. Your mate can, and probably will, respond by saying, "That's not true," and you will be involved in an argument. On the other hand, if you say, "I feel as if I'm not getting enough help from you with the children," your mate cannot argue about the way you feel. You have given some information about yourself that your mate cannot refute. The discussion is then open for a resolution of your problem, that is, the way you feel.

Avoid telling other persons what they are doing, thinking, or feeling. They know better than you what they are about. Avoid useless arguments and resolve problems quickly and painlessly by giving information only about yourself. Begin statements with words like "I feel . . .," "I believe . . .," "I hope . . .," "I want . . .," "I think . . .," "I am . . .," "It seems to me . . .," "I plan . . .," "I need . . .," "I would like . . .," and "I expect. . . ." Rather than saying to a child, "You are really making me mad," you'll be more effective saying, "I'm getting mad. I want you to do. . . ."

Here is an example: "I am disappointed in the way you cleaned the kitchen. I expected you to wipe off the cupboards and sweep the floor." This is more effective than, "Johnny, you didn't do a good job in the kitchen," because Johnny is immediately provoked to a defense of himself. He may say, "I did too," and you then have the job of trying to convince him his beliefs are wrong. The time, the argument, and the feelings are all out of proportion with the significance of the issue. But Johnny cannot argue about your being disappointed or about what you expected. If he understands your feelings and still does not finish the job, you have an obedience problem, but the issue is not clouded by argument.

Focusing On The Problem

In limiting your communications to information about yourself, you fix attention on the actual problem and its solution. If you present the difficulty as your problem, the other person must decide either to help you solve your problem or to let you know she/he is not interested. Either way, the issues are clear-cut, and you have information upon which to base further action. If you say to your mate, "I have a problem. I am not satisfied with our sex life," your mate must respond to the problem as you have defined it, that is, your sexual dissatisfaction. But if you say to your mate, "You are not a good sex partner," you have not defined a problem, you have only made an accusation, which your partner may dispute. Your partner, however, cannot dispute your claim of being dissatisfied.

The Rhetorical Question?

Some questions carry an implied attitude or a statement about the other person.

A rhetorical question, for instance, is one for which the speaker already knows the answer. It is asked not to get information, but to trap the other person into an admission of error or wrongdoing. If the person answers directly, he exposes himself to humiliation or intolerable demands. His usual recourse, therefore, is to evade the question, or to lie. An insincere question usually receives an insincere answer. As a result, the discussion disintegrates into a meaningless game of cat and mouse. Ask a question for information, not as a preliminary for a demand.

I overheard the following conversation between a stepfather and his stepdaughter one day. The man wanted his stepdaughter to stop seeing a certain boy.

SF. "How long have you been dating Bill?"

D. "I don't know. What difference does it make to you?"

SF. "Don't get smart with me, I asked a simple question and I want a simple answer."

D. "Ten years."

SF. "You're only fourteen. You started seeing him last Christmas."

D. "So why did you ask?"

SF. "Oh, I can't do anything with you. You're grounded for a week."

This stepfather's use of the rhetorical question led him away from his original intent; instead, he entered a power struggle with the teenager. He apparently thought he could get her to condemn herself by her own admissions, but she never let him get past his first clumsy attempt. She already knew what his purpose was, and she neatly sidestepped him. She would still not give up her boyfriend.

The stepfather could have been much more successful had he approached the matter something like this:

SF.   "Wendy, you have been seeing Bill since last Christmas. I must insist you stop seeing him."

D.   "You can't tell me who I can see and who I can't. "

SF.   "I can, and I am. I expect you to break off your relationship with the boy. If you don't do it, yourself, I will talk with the boy and his parents and let them know my feelings. Should you continue to see him on a dating basis, I will devise some other ways to let you know I mean business. This is the end of this discussion for now. Make your own choice about how you are going to break off the relationship."

The girl, while not liking the directness of

this approach, has no opportunity to confuse the issues. She must respond directly. There may be further trouble ahead, but no obscuring of the real issue.

To effectively communicate, make statements that give information about yourself only, and ask questions that provide only information you need to form statements about yourself.

Rule 4: Know When Agreement Is Impossible

Effective communication does not necessarily mean agreement. It is important to be able to distinguish between understanding and agreement. After you are sure that you and the other person are working from mutually understood assumptions and that you have clearly understood each other's information or request, you still may not get what you want, or you may be unwilling to do what the other wants. At these times, discussion is no longer fruitful and may be dangerous. Make a habit of knowing when there is nothing left to say, and stop talking.

Rule 5: Make Your Tone Agree With Your Words

People pay as much attention to how others say things as to what they say. Spoken communication and the unspoken communication accompanying it must match to be effective. Body language, eye contact, and tone of voice are powerful communicators, often more powerful than the spoken word.

The converse of this rule is also true: use the words that agree with your feelings. If your words accurately describe your thinking and feeling, they have great impact on your listener.

What we call tact is a process of obscuring our true feelings by our use of words with pleasant connotations. I am not suggesting you abandon tactfulness; it is the balm that soothes potentially abrasive situations that are not important enough to risk injured feelings. I am suggesting that, if you have the ability and the courage to say what you feel in precisely the manner that you feel it, you have the means for powerful communication.

The Power Of Sincerity

True feelings are disclosed by the subtlest shifts in mood and tone of voice. Children seem peculiarly keen to these shifts. They trust or distrust with uncanny accuracy. If they distrust you, they withhold a part of themselves from you so that communication is sporadic and guarded. If they trust you, however, they respond to you freely and spontaneously. Communication then flows easily.

That is the key to communicating with children: absolute sincerity. There is a special power in sincere communications. All of our experience with sincere people seems like one consistent event. What they say is congruent with how they feel. There is no confusion. We never have to guess at anything.

When You Fake It

If you give your stepchild a kiss and a hug when you would really rather kiss and hug a snake, the stepchild will only consider you a pretty good faker. You will not fool him into believing you love him. Some thoughts, of course, you will do well to keep to yourself for the sake of harmony. Understand, however, that if you are faking a communication or relationship, the best you can hope for is a fake response.

Children, and people in general, will trust you to the same degree that what you say matches with the way you say it. Your body, eyes, and voice will give you away every time you say something that does not reflect how you feel. People may not be able to judge what you really mean, but they will sense that you are hiding something.

Saying What You Mean And Meaning What You Say

You can get your stepchildren to reciprocate in an honest relationship by taking their words at face value. Tell your stepchildren that you will be honest in the expression of your needs and that you expect them to be honest about their needs. Then act on whatever verbal information they give you. If they are in the habit of obscuring their needs and wants with evasive language, they will soon discover that they need to speak clearly and powerfully with you to get their needs known and met. In effect, you say to them, "If you will consistently tell me what you want and need from me as honestly as you know how, I will consistently be honest with you about whether I can, or am willing, to meet your needs and wants."

You will thus take the guesswork out of your relationship. If you choose to be effective in your communications, say what you mean. If you choose to be tactful, know that your communication will be obscured and that most people will understand you are trying to be tactful.

Summary

If you will adopt and use the principles of communication discussed in this chapter, you will have communication tools to build and strengthen any relationship, especially with stepchildren. Of the scores of ideas and principles you can use to develop finesse in your style of communicating, these are the basics:

1. Never assume.
2. Plan what you want to say.
3. Give information only about yourself.
4. Know when agreement is impossible.
5. Make your tone agree with your words.

Chapter 5

HOW TO HANDLE THEM

There are some common, recognizable patterns to the ways children manage to exasperate adults, especially stepparents. In this chapter, I will describe some of the tactics you may be encountering, and I will suggest effective ways to deal with kids who use the tactics. As we look at these tactics, remember that you need not be concerned with the emotions that produce them. You are dealing with behavior only. Improving the behavior is the sole means you have to create a better relationship, unless some solid form of bonding occurs, which is unlikely. Avoid long, involved discussions of each other's feelings. Feelings are best dealt with after you already have a good working basis of mutually acceptable behavior.

Direct Disobedience

The most obvious form of behavioral problem is direct disobedience. When you ask or tell a child to do something and the child refuses, you have disobedience. The flow of your wishes is blocked by the direct refusal of the child to comply. The key word is "direct." Disobedience comes in many forms, but for now, I'm talking only about direct, clear-cut refusal to comply with your wishes.

It is important to your effectiveness to be able to identify clearly the problem you are encountering. Direct disobedience has three characteristics: (1) Your desire is clearly stated and clearly understood, (2) the child verbally refuses, and (3) the child physically does not comply with your request or demand. For example, if you tell a child to feed the dog, and the child says, "No," and refuses to feed the dog, you have direct disobedience on your hands. Awareness of this will help you determine your options.

Deal With The Issue, Not The Child

When you have a clear-cut case of direct disobedience, deal with the matter in question, not with the child. This is crucial. If you deal only with the matter in question, you have a chance of getting your demand met; but, if you begin dealing with the child, you create the potential for getting into a personality-based power struggle that you are unlikely to win. Your task is to tailor your response to achieving acceptable behavior. More about this later.

Provide Alternative Behaviors

Set boundaries on the conflict, by defining acceptable alternative behavior. Give the child choices. A dialogue between you and the child might go like this:

You. "Mary, please feed the dog."

Child. "No."

You. "The dog needs to be fed within the next five minutes, and you are the one to do it."

Child. "I'm not going to do it."

You. "Here are your choices, Mary. You may feed the dog within the next five minutes, or you may spend one hour sitting at the kitchen table, facing the wall."

Child. "I want to go over to Bobby's and play."

You. "That is not one of your choices right now. You may either feed the dog in the next four minutes, or you may spend one hour sitting at the kitchen table facing the wall."

Child. "You can't make me do anything."

You. "Your choices are to feed the dog in the next three and one-half minutes, or spend an hour sitting at the kitchen table facing the wall. Which do you choose to do?"

Child. "You're always trying to make me do things."

You. "Your choice is to feed the dog or sit at the table facing the wall. Which is it going to be?"

Child. "Oh, all right. Then can I go to Bobby's?"

You. "Sure."

You may be skeptical, but, I assure you, if you will limit your discussion with a directly disobedient child to the matter in question, you will succeed in getting your wishes met most of the time.

One note: Be sure the alternative you set is within the child's capability. A twelve-year-old is capable of sitting for an hour, but a five-year-old may not be. Perhaps fifteen minutes would be enough. If you make the alternatives too stringent, you set yourself up for another struggle. Do not use a cannon when a cork gun will do the job. Remember, the issue is not that the child has disobeyed. The issue is that the child has made a choice of her own free will, and the family expects the child to accept the consequences of her choice.

Let The Child Make The Choice

Notice in the above discussion what you accomplished and what you avoided. First, you set forth clear choices for the child. They were choices the child emphatically had to make. Most importantly, they were choices that have nothing to do with you. By your own steadfastness, you created a situation in which all responsibility for choice rested with the child.

Keeping Your Relationship Out Of The Discussion

That brings us to the second thing you did; you refused the child's attempt to put you into the conversation. You avoided getting into an argument about your authority, and you avoided a discussion of your history of dealing with her. If you had allowed the child to dwell on these topics, you would have lost the power and direction of your purpose. As it was, you simply would not let the child get off the subject.

Here's how that discussion might have gone if you had not been careful:

You. "Mary, please feed the dog."

Child. "No."

You. "The dog needs to be fed, and you are the one to do it."

Child. "I'm not going to do it."
(Here's where you can really mess up.)

You. "Don't tell me what you are going to do and not do. I want you to feed that dog this minute. If you don't, I'll spank you."

Child. "You better not. You're not my mother (father), and I don't have to do anything you say."

You. "Oh, Mary, why can't we just be friends? I get so tired of arguing with you."

Child. "I hate you. I don't want to be your friend. Why don't you go away and leave me alone?"

You. "I'm going to tell your father about this."

Child. "See if I care. He loves me."

You can see the difference. You have allowed the nature of your relationship with the child to become the issue. If you allow yourself to be drawn into personality and authority issues, you're dead. The child diverts you from the matter at hand and leaves you at the mercy of your own guilt feelings. All you are left with is the hope that your spouse can do something about the relationship. Child: 1. Stepparent and Dog: Zero.

When All Else Fails

What do you do when, for about the tenth time, this doesn't work? If you have set clear choices, and the child has not responded properly (let's say she bolts out the door), let the matter rest until you have your spouse present for added power. Continue to let the child know she has made a choice, and do not waiver in your demand that the choice will be acted out. When your spouse arrives, insist, if you must, that he back you up when you tell the child to spend one hour sitting at the kitchen table facing the wall. Explain the situation, demand cooperation, then say to the child: "Mary, earlier today you chose to spend one hour sitting at the kitchen table facing the wall. Now you get to do it. Sit down."

Get Your Spouse's Agreement

Do not ask your spouse to handle the matter; do it yourself. If you must offer further, less desirable choices, do so. But you probably won't have to. Insist that your spouse intervene only to convince the child that he or she has made a choice, but handle the matter yourself.

The business of getting your spouse to cooperate is often a little ticklish. There is a simple way around this. When you are offering limited choices to a child, keep the least attractive alternative at a level the spouse will accept. If you insist the child be grounded for a week or severely spanked for a minor infraction, your spouse might not agree to back you. If your alternatives are reasonable, your spouse is more inclined to cooperate. Then, the child will understand that she cannot play her natural parent against you.

A Recap

In cases of direct disobedience:
1. Deal with the issue, not the child.
2. Provide alternative behaviors.
3. Let the child make the choice.
4. Keep your relationship out of the discussion.
5. Have your spouse's agreement on the alternative you've set.

Passive-Aggressive Behavior

Unfortunately, most child management problems are not so clearly drawn as direct disobedience. Misbehavior often takes a subtle, difficult form called passive-aggression. Passive-aggression is misbehavior that avoids direct confrontation. It has an irking quality of inertia about. It is inaction rather than action—something that apparently has satisfied a demand but actually has not. It has an attitudinal flavor about it that seems at once cooperative and defiant. It is behavior designed to irritate you, to keep you emotionally and intellectually off-balance, and to make you react to petty things until you begin to think something is wrong with yourself.

Some Examples, Historical and Otherwise

In its extreme form, passive-aggression is a refusal to do anything at all. Ghandi wrested India from the British by doing absolutely nothing. He and his followers wouldn't fight, wouldn't argue, wouldn't eat. They did, however, paralyze the Indian economy by lying in the streets and across railroad tracks. These tactics forced the British into ugly reaction, which had the effect of popularizing Ghandi's cause. Finally, the British capitulated under the weight of massive social resistance and adverse public opinion.

The anti-war movement of the 1960's was successful largely because of passive-aggression. The demonstrators staged sit-ins. They didn't do much, just sat where the government didn't want them until the government reacted. If a riot broke out, the demonstrators legitimately claimed they had been attacked. The government was placed in the position of having to defend itself for aggressing against its own citizens, who, ostensibly, were quietly sitting in a public place. That was a hard act to defend, no matter what you thought of the war in Vietnam.

Closer to home, passive-aggression shows up in behavior like your stepchild's feeding the dog, but not giving it water; bringing you the soft drink you asked for, in a dirty glass; doing all the dishes, except for one pan; agreeing to rake the lawn, and leaving one small pile of grass. When you ask your teenager to stop cracking his knuckles, and he does stop for five minutes, then gives you a knuckle symphony on his way out of the room, he is giving you a dose of passive-aggression. You're being passively aggressed against when you tell the eight-year-old to go put some shoes on, and he comes back with the shoes on the wrong feet.

Passive-aggression has the quality of leaving you not quite sure whether you have been deliberately disobeyed and insulted, or whether you have made some error in expectation or judgment. When you ask your stepchild to turn down the stereo and he lowers the volume a barely perceptible fraction of a decibel, you may not know whether to thank the child for compliance or raise a fuss about being defied. When you tell the children to stop running in the house, and they come charging back through at a 20 mph walk, you've been had. You're in an awkward spot when you have told a child to stop throwing the ball in the house, and two minutes later you hear the regular pounding of the ball against the outside of the kitchen wall.

An Extreme Case

A determined child can drive you to distraction, if you're not careful, by simply doing nothing or resolutely doing something aggravating. A certain nine-year-old would come to the dinner table, but steadfastly refuse to eat anything his stepmother prepared. He would eat whatever his father made, but nothing else. I know a seventeen-year-old who, if refused the keys to the family car, would stare balefully and steadily at his mother and stepfather. He would follow them about the house and continue his staring until they gave him the keys or took refuge in a bedroom, where they could lock the door.

These extreme forms of passive-aggression usually represent pathology in the family, which should be dealt with professionally. Most passive-aggression, though, you can deal with yourself, if you know what is happening and are prepared to take the necessary steps to correct it.

The Motive Behind Passive-Aggression

Passive-aggression, unlike direct disobedience, is a statement about your relationship with the child. The child's objective is to make your life miserable, to keep you emotionally off-balance by concealing his disobedience behind minimally good behavior. It represents an unwillingness to be engaged with you in a productive relationship. It is designed to let you know who is in control. In effect, the passive-aggressive child is saying: "You may have some control over what I do, but you are at my mercy because I can always find a way to prevent you from feeling good about anything you do with me."

The Operating Principles

Dealing with passive-aggressive behavior requires that you understand the principles upon which it operates. First, the perpetrator understands that you want something done or have a desire that is important to you. The more important it is to you, the more leverage the perpetrator has in defeating you. Second, the perpetrator relies on the belief that you will confine your reactions to predictable patterns. In other words, you must play the game in order for the game to work. Moreover, the perpetrator believes you will play the game fairly, while he does not. Third, the perpetrator assumes he has more stamina than you.

Dealing With Passive-Aggression

In broad terms, the way to effectively deal with passive-aggressive behavior is to refuse to comply with the operating principles of passive-aggression.

First, check yourself carefully to see whether the goal is worth the effort. If it's not, abandon the idea. Be careful: any time you abandon a desire to passive-aggression, it encourages more of the same, because the kid now has evidence that he does, indeed, have more stamina than you. It's usually better to hang in there until you have accomplished what you want.

Second, and here is the real key, do not accept the principle that you have to react in a predictable way. Do not play by the rules of the game. Act, don't react. Take the lead in the game and keep changing the rules until the perpetrator figures out he is gaining nothing.

Third, do not accept the idea you can't stick with it.

There is another important element to dealing with passive-aggression. Never use force. When you use force, you are only telling a child you are beaten and out of creative options. Soon the force becomes part of the pattern, and children become immune to it. If a child has a special interest in making you miserable, spanking will do nothing to change the pattern. Recognize the pattern of a passive-aggressive interaction, determine how you fit into the pattern, then change your behavior. Since force is a predictable outcome of your frustration, it plays into the hands of the passive-aggressive child. Instead, change the pattern and change the rules. Then, instead of triumphing over you, the child is playing catch-up with you.

Two Successful Examples

Example 1—A young wife, who had two stepchildren, 14 and 10, was a fastidious housekeeper; however, the children were continually leaving their clothes lying around the house, especially in their bedroom. For months she set a daily pattern of demands and complaints, escalating on occasion to spankings and bitter words.

Her husband, their natural father, would not involve himself in the matter, grumbling that he didn't see what there was to raise such a fuss about. This particularly irritated the stepmother, because whenever the children sensed she was going to try to involve their father, the clothes would miraculously disappear from view.

The kids were getting to her. They subtly but effectively taunted her, and at the same time they were undermining their father's faith in her ability to maintain composure. The days were getting hard to endure. She began to resign herself to picking up their stuff herself, just so it would get done. She was miserable.

Then one day, she decided not to play their game anymore. She announced one morning that she would continue to pick up their clothes, but that she was going to throw them up into a topmost cabinet shelf in the hall. And she began to do just that. Each day she would gather up anything lying about and throw it in the hall shelf. When the children began to run out of things to wear, she told them they were welcome to get their stuff from the closet. So, daily they climbed upon a chair and pulled out what they needed; however, they still left piles of clothes in the hall. They were not about to give up.

After about two weeks, she said nothing to them at all, but began to put their stuff in a topmost, unused cupboard in the kitchen. The children could no longer find their clothes in the hall and asked her where they were. She replied it was a secret, but they were welcome to hunt for them. Instead of hunting, they wore what they had left until both children were down to almost nothing.

The husband had been told of her plan and was noncommittal at first; but he began to get concerned when the children could not appear in school looking fresh the way they had. His response was to demand that his wife produce the clothing for the children. Some angry words were spoken, but the upshot of it was, she told her husband that he, too, was welcome to hunt for the children's clothing. For herself, she would continue to pick up anything out of its proper place, put it wherever her imagination directed, and that was that. She declared that she would be happy to wash and fold any clothing she found in the laundry hamper. She would place the folded clothing on the children's beds, and the children could put them away. Anything found still out the next day, however, would continue to disappear.

Exasperated, the father ordered the children to hunt until they found their clothes and henceforth to keep them where they belonged. The stepmother kept her promises, and the issue was eventually settled.

What she had done was break out of the game the children were playing. They assumed, rightly for a long time, that their stepmother could not allow herself to see them poorly, inadequately dressed. They also assumed that they had the tacit blessing of their father for their behavior.

Then, the stepmother stopped playing by their rules and changed the pattern. The children could no longer predict the stepmother's reactions. They soon found that their father was telling them to do what their stepmother had wanted all along.

Example 2—A nine-year-old refused to eat his stepmother's meals. The pattern in the family was for the entire family to sit down to dinner. The boy's father insisted that the boy join them. This much the boy was willing to do. It gave his behavior more impact because everyone was there to observe it. Every meal time was a tense, excruciatingly painful affair. The parents would plead, cajole, try humor, try logic, threaten, and finally lose their temper.

Every three days or so, the father would get so angry he would strike the boy and send him off to his room. Nevertheless, the boy remained mute, sullen, and would not eat. Eventually, the father would prepare something for fear the boy would become undernourished.

The boy's motives were not particularly important, but his behavior was tearing the family apart. The boy knew his father would not let him starve, didn't care about the periodic beatings, and was successfully driving a wedge between the father and stepmother. It seemed an impossible situation.

The supper issue got resolved in the following way. It was the father's habit to rise early and fix breakfast for the family. He had done it for the years before his remarriage and had continued the practice. Then one day, he added something new to the pattern. Each morning, having finished frying bacon, the father cooked one hamburger in the bacon grease. This he wrapped in waxed paper and put in the refrigerator. Each evening when the father arrived home, he spanked the boy lightly three times, then told him to go out and play. When the boy asked what the spanking was for, the father always said these exact words: "I had a hard day. I won't have much energy later." When suppertime came, the stepmother would serve the rest of the family whatever she had fixed, but place the cold hamburger on the boy's otherwise empty plate. Thereafter, the boy's eating habits were completely ignored. No pleading, asking, threatening, or beating.

For most of the week, the boy defiantly ate

the hamburger. Toward the end of the week, he would not eat the cold, greasy hamburger any more. He was still getting lightly spanked for no reason well before supper, his father was fixing him a hamburger in the morning to be eaten cold at supper, and the family was otherwise ignoring his eating habits.

Toward the beginning of the second week, the boy took a piece of lettuce from a salad his stepmother had fixed. No one paid any attention. The hamburger and before-dinner light spanking continued. By the middle of the week, the boy was openly taking small portions of food the stepmother had fixed. Still no one seemed to pay any attention. At the end of the second week, the boy came to the table and, seeing the hambrger, shouted, "It's not fair."

"What's not fair?" asked the stepmother.

"Nobody ever talks to me anymore," pouted the boy.

"Why, we'll be glad to talk with you any time you like, if you have something interesting to talk about," said the father.

The boy said he didn't like cold hamburgers, and the father replied he was not interested in talking about food. He would continue to fix a hamburger every morning, unless his son asked him to stop.

"Other than that," said the father, "you're

welcome to eat anything you like. It's up to you. But I won't talk about food anymore."

Then the boy said he didn't want to get spanked any more.

"Okay," the father replied, "I'm glad you spoke up."

So, the problem was solved. The parents had done several important things. They had interrupted the pattern of the frustrating behavior in such a way it no longer made any sense to the boy. They had backed out of the personal power struggle with the boy by no longer allowing themselves to be upset by his refusal to eat the stepmother's meals; yet, they let the child know they would not let him go hungry. And they had put it into the child's hands to make his own choices about how he was going to be treated and behave. This was strongly reinforced by the father's simple agreement to stop spanking the child when asked to do so. Unlike direct confrontations where the food would remain the issue, the family dealt with the matter by establishing their own level of emotional engagement with the child.

Remember that passive-aggressive behavior is designed to affect the emotional tone of a relationship; it is not necessarily task-oriented. It therefore needs to be dealt with primarily with an understanding of its emotional flavor.

Moving Toward Your Own Solution

The foregoing examples may sound a little cold and manipulative. You may have noticed that I have not suggested you sit down and talk with a child about feelings or try to understand the motives behind his behavior. There is a very simple reason for this. To put it bluntly, feelings don't count for anything until you and the child have established mutually acceptable behavioral patterns. When it is your feelings that are being attacked, there is no point in holding up your wounds for examination in the hope you will receive mercy or create guilt. I can't imagine you would willingly accept anybody's pity, nor can you expect to get far trading on anyone else's guilt.

Control Your Feelings—There is a principle to understand here. Nobody can make you feel anything. You are the only person in the world who has control over the way you feel. Someone may do something intended to frustrate you, but it is only you who can make yourself angry. A child cannot make you feel guilty. A child can try to make you feel guilty, but it will only work if you allow yourself to feel the guilt. The same is true with your whole range of feelings, including love and affection.

When you can accept that principle, you can also learn to remain emotionally neutral with respect to a difficult situation. Not necessarily indifferent, just neutral. You can allow yourself to be curious about whatever efforts the child is making, to examine the pattern of your relationship with the child and to use your intellect rather than your emotions to develop a plan for more productive dealings.

I know a stepmother who for a year had been dreadfully annoyed by what she perceived as her stepdaughter's unyielding demands on her time and attention during weekend visits. When she backed off from her annoyance for a while and examined the situation as a pattern in which she was involved, she concluded that the child was not making negative demands. Rather, the child seemed to be trying very hard to assure the stepmother that she was loved, cared for, and accepted. The child was showing affection for the stepmother in the only way she knew, by drawing and coloring pictures as gifts and bringing them to the stepmother, thereby creating excuses to exchange hugs, kisses, and words of appreciation. Understanding this, the stepmother was able to modify, in a positive way, both her own and the stepchild's behavior.

The purpose of any interaction with a child is ultimately the enhancement of the quality of your own life. That you have a stepchild to take into account is only one of many factors you must take for granted as you shape your world to suit you. Unless you really enjoy being frustrated, angry, or otherwise upset, you can control the way you handle most incidents to increase the potential for feeling good about yourself and the child. If you will consistently take a rational approach to your dealings with stepchildren, you have the opportunity to short-circuit the effects of passive-aggressive behavior. But, if you allow such behavior to get you upset and off-balanced, you'll have a very difficult time thinking your way to a new pattern of interaction.

Play The What If Game—When you are experiencing passive-aggressive behavior from a child, treat it as a curiosity. Be curious enough to notice how you are reacting to whatever the child is or is not doing. Examine the pattern carefully, then see if you can find a way to act that changes the pattern.

One handy little device for doing this is to play the game of What If with yourself. When you're not deeply involved in your own frustration, give yourself some time to sit down with a pencil and paper. Write at the top, "I am interested in enhancing the quality of my life. I notice I become (name the feeling) when (child's name) does (name the behavior). What if I . . .?"

As you list things after the "what if" section,

let your creativity roll. Write down anything that comes to mind, no matter how outrageous it seems. Be particularly attentive to things that seem impossible for you. Anything you would normally not do is probably the very thing you should try. If you know there are things you would not expect yourself to do, so does the child. As long as you restrict the range of your feelings and behavior, the child can count on those limitations to control you. How many times have you rehashed an encounter with some body and wished you had said or done something other than what you did? Next time, do it. There will be a next time, if the pattern is a consistent one, so you'll have the opportunity.

Your curiosity sheet may look something like this: I am interested in enhancing the quality of my life. I notice I become angry when Bobby gets up every five minutes after he is put to bed. What if I:

Get angrier?

Spank him?

Do a somersault every time he comes into the room?

Tell him not to go back to bed?

Put him to bed later?

Put him to bed earlier?

Go to bed myself?

Laugh loud and long each time he gets up?

Ignore him?

Talk to him for a long time?

Give him a 45-minute lecture each time he gets up?

Have him take a bath every time he gets up?

Ask him to put on his clothes and do a chore each time he gets up.

See to it there is a glass of water in his bedroom?

Make a recording on a tape machine with all my normal responses, then simply push the button whenever he gets up?

Give him ten arithmetic problems to do before he can go back to bed?

Refer all interactions with him to my spouse?

Go visit him in his room every four minutes?

Your list may go on and on. All that is important is that anything you come up with be different from what you're already doing.

Choose a Course of Action—From your What If list, choose a course of action to break the deadlock. It will probably not make much difference what you finally choose, as long as it works. Once you decide upon a new course of action, stick with it for long enough to determine whether it is working or not. Two weeks is usually long enough for a good assessment.

To determine whether something is working, check yourself to see if you are still getting angry, and check to see if the child's behavior is changing. You may achieve results in both areas. Even if you only find you are no longer getting angry, count that as a success and be satisfied with it. You'll probably discover that as soon as you begin to take a new course of action, your unpleasant feeling will begin to dissipate. Most bad feelings result from your belief that you are powerless to change something. As soon as you prove to yourself that you do have options, anger will dissolve in the face of your new behavior.

Disagreement and Argument

There is a class of frustrating behavior that is neither disobedience nor passive-aggressive behavior. It is simple disagreement and argument. Just as you, children have beliefs and opinions about the world and their proper place in it. They may be ill-informed and lack depth of understanding, but they are no less sure of their views than you are of yours. Your views and theirs often conflict, and you have disagreements and arguments.

Confusion With Other Forms of Behavior

It is important to distinguish between simple disagreement, on one hand, and disobedience or passive-aggressive behavior on the other. The adolescent who refuses to babysit for his little sister may be doing so as a result of his belief that such behavior is beneath his dignity, rather than a matter of challenging your authority. A twelve-year-old girl may refuse to participate in physical education classes as a matter of modesty, rather than as a challenge to the authority of the school. Sometimes, what appears to be disobedience or passive-aggressive behavior, is actually behavior based on the child's belief that you can't or won't understand his viewpoint. He therefore acts without explanation.

Where Children Get Their Ideas

If you had the opportunity to examine the sources of children's knowledge, beliefs, and opinions, you'd probably be amazed at how little influence you, and even the child's natural parents, have on them. Schools, churches, and peers rank as the primary sources of information and value formation for children. Parents and stepparents usually enter the picture only at the extreme ends of the child's experience. When you send your child to school, you tacitly insist the child mold himself to the behavior and beliefs the school promotes, without really knowing what they are. When you send a child to Sunday school or take him to church, you have little way of knowing what the child chooses to accept and believe. A child's friends and peers form the community within which he tests his beliefs and ways of viewing the world. If he receives acceptance of his views from his peers, he is not likely to check much further for validation, particularly with adults.

Most adults are profoundly surprised at the things their children understand and believe, that is, when they take the time to discover their children's beliefs. The entertainer, Art Linkletter, understood and exploited this reality in an engaging form of entertainment. You will do well to remember that kids not only say the darnedest things, they believe them too.

The Hidden Basis of Some Disagreements

The following is not a common problem, but it is illustrative. An eight-year-old boy unaccountably began wetting and soiling himself. He had been appropriately toilet trained by the time he was four, and there seemed to be no particular family or other stress which would bring about this odd behavior. His mother and stepfather were very concerned, trying all sorts of remedies from pleadings to spankings, with no success. The boy would promise not to do it again, then turn up wet and soiled. When his family brought the boy to me, convinced he was emotionally disturbed, the boy and I got lucky and resolved the problem in ten minutes.

Pete. "I'd like to know why you can't use the bathroom anymore like you used to."

Boy. "It's bad."

Pete. "What's bad?"

Boy. (embarrassed and flushing) "To touch myself there. (pointing to his genitals)"

Pete. "How do you know that?"

Boy. "Mrs. Jones said so."

Pete. "Who is Mrs. Jones?"

Boy. "My teacher."

Pete. "If I were to tell you it's all right to touch yourself there when you go to the bathroom, would you believe me?"

Boy. (Shakes his head no)

Pete. "Would you believe her?"

Boy. (Eagerly) "Yes."

I called Mrs. Jones on the phone right then. I explained the problem and asked her to assure the boy it was all right to touch himself when he went to the bathroom. She did, and the problem was resolved.

As it turned out, his teacher had observed him scratching himself in school about a month before and severely admonished him, telling him never to do it again. The poor little fellow generalized the admonition, and, no matter how hard he tried, he could not succeed in using the toilet without touching himself. School had let out for the summer a couple of days later; and the little boy was left with the choice of being bad according to a teacher he loved or of being misunderstood and soiling himself. He chose to be misunderstood rather than be bad, according to his perceptions. When his mother and stepfather would scold him for soiling himself, the boy would cry and repeat, "It's bad, it's bad," and the parents assumed he meant he was agreeing with them that to soil himself was bad.

In this case the disagreement was covert. The boy had a belief which was not known to the rest of the family. The more common type of disagreement is a direct, verbal argument.

Four Traps In Disagreement And Argument

Whenever you are in disagreement with a child, there are some basic traps you can easily fall into if you're not careful. One of them is anger that there is a disagreement at all. A disagreement is essentially a divergence of thinking processes. If you react to a disagreement emotionally, you demonstrate to a child that you are incapable of thinking calmly and constructively. You show the child that you value your prejudices more than sound thought, and that you have no objective information to give him. If the child is to discuss things with you he will have to adopt your prejudices, or else refrain from trying out his thinking on you. You also lose your opportunity to impress the child as a person of thought and depth.

The second trap is the assumption that, because you are an adult, your beliefs and attitudes must be right, whereas a child's must be wrong, unless he agrees with you. When you do that, you set yourself up as being perfect, a ridiculous posture. The child can only conclude you are a liar or a fool, maybe both. As a result, a child may automatically dismiss all of your beliefs.

A third trap is the insistence that a child agree with you on all matters. Although you may legitimately expect a child to behave the way you want him to, insisting that a child agree with your reasons for wanting that behavior will frustrate you and teach the child to lie about his beliefs. This is not to say you shouldn't try to persuade a child to share your beliefs, if you think they will serve the child well now and in the future. On the other hand, the child may not be able to accept your beliefs, in which case he can only pretend to agree if you insist.

A fourth trap is the assumption that you and the child have the same basic beliefs and conceptual values. When these differ, arguments tend to become circular, interminable, and frustrating. The section of this book on communication will help you recognize false assumptions operating between you and a child.

Disagreement and Argument As A Healthful Process

Disagreement and argument are the starting points for almost all growth in mutual understanding. Any contrast in views is a tremendously healthful experience for a child, because it provides an opportunity for exercising rational thought. If a child will behave, but not agree with you, accept the behavior and leave the disagreement alone. Respect the child's right to have opinions of his own, just as you expect a child to respect yours.

General Household Discipline

So far I have been talking about fairly extreme forms of child management problems. The more extreme a management problem is, the more creative you need to be to resolve it. But most of the time you are engaged in the day-to-day business of living with your stepchildren, whether full-time or on visitation schedules. This requires a routine system of discipline to keep things running smoothly.

Discipline, in the way I use the term, does not mean punishment; rather, discipline is an orderly, productive way of conducting life's business. It is a set of expectations for both yourself and your stepchildren by which you train each other to live in harmony. For the most part, you set the expectations, and the children are responsible for complying with them.

Discipline is synonymous with orderliness, the moving smoothly from one event to the next in daily life. Orderliness of this kind requires a fairly high level of cooperation among all the people in your household. Cooperation is not obtained by force or threat; it is the result of people making voluntary choices that are compatible with their own needs and the needs of the rest of the family.

Good Discipline From Good Expectations

Good discipline in your household has its roots in the nature, strength, and quality of your expectations. It's almost a psychic phenomenon. If you truly expect harmony and discipline, you will probably get it. If you expect to be hassled, disobeyed, and defied, you probably will be.

The Formula For Good Discipline

You will achieve good discipline if you stick with the following formula.

1. Make your expectations clear and firm.
2. As much as possible, remain emotionally detached from your expectations. Maintain your sense of humor.
3. When your expectations are challenged, give the children choices between meeting your expectations and doing less desirable things.
4. Insist that the children make their choices wholly on their own.
5. Insist that they hold themselves responsible for their choices.
6. Never get involved in a power struggle with the children as you are working toward discipline; just give them choices and insist they choose one.
7. Avoid extremes.

You've already seen how these ideas work against severe disciplinary problems. You will find them just as helpful in keeping routine discipline in your home.

You eliminate power struggles with children by presenting your expectations of disciplinary order in a way that gives them a clear choice between cooperation and less desirable options. When they do cooperate, all of you can feel good about it. If they opt for a less desirable alternative, the choice rests entirely with the child, and you need only insist that the child accept the consequences of his decision. You should never have to be in a position of punishing a child.

When a child deliberately disobeys you, give him a choice of consequences: "Mary, you were to be home by six o'clock and you're late. To help you remember to be on time, you may either mop the kitchen floor or scrub the bathroom tub. Which do you prefer?" In other words, create choices that have merit in their own right and that can give the child a sense of accomplishment. There are always any number of necessary, but relatively unpleasant, chores around the house. Turn them to advantage as your disciplinary alternatives. "Bobby, you may choose to catch the school bus on time this morning, or you may choose to have me take you to school. If I take you, then you do two loads of laundry when you return home this afternoon."

When a child chooses the alternate option you have given, accept that choice without question. Simply make whatever explanations the child needs to carry out his choice, then compliment him for whatever he accomplishes. You don't need to get angry at him for making the choice you did not prefer. You would not get angry at anyone else you were trying to help. In fact, you can both feel good about the whole business.

The consistent use of this method of discipline generates mutual respect between you and the child. The child chooses, is aware that you have respected his choice, even if it seems a crummy one to you, and you can respect his accomplishment and his decision-making. It's a clever system and it works.

Another advantage is that the system does not necessarily require the cooperation of your spouse. Many natural parents, either unwittingly or deliberately, will undermine the stepparent's efforts to assume authority and disciplinary control over the children. In this case, however, a natural parent can hardly object to your giving the child realistic, non-threatening choices about his behavior.

At times, of course, something needs to be done urgently, and there is no time for choices. Those times are pretty rare, but they do occur. If you have been consistent with the style of discipline I'm suggesting over a period of time, you can usually simply state that there is no choice. This is when the quality and strength of your disciplining are tested. If you have gained the cooperation and respect of your children, you will have the pleasure of seeing them accept your demand without question.

A Word About Physical Punishment

Stay away from physical force, such as spanking. The threat of a spanking permits no range of constructive choices. It is punishment, nothing more. It does nothing to improve the quality of the relationship.

I do not object to spanking on moral or ethical grounds. I recognize there are times when a parent must forcibly get a child's attention. But to use physical threat as a normal style of getting cooperation leads to a cycle of fear and reprisal. Repeated use of force simply doesn't work in the long run. You may get a level of submission from a child, but it will be a sullen, uncooperative kind of submission. Worse, you prevent the growth of any kind of positive feelings toward each other. Relying on corporal punishment leads to anger and frustration. Who needs it? Your life is too short to waste time being mad at somebody else's kid.

The better way to manage children is to place responsibility for their behavior on themselves, rather than on yourself. This works at all age levels, from the toddler on up, particularly adolescents. They may be bigger than you are; spanking is absolutely out of the question.

Distinguishing Between Child and Behavior

There is a difference between what the child does and who the child is. A bad child does not exist. One may act badly, by all means, but that doesn't mean he is intrinsically bad. A child is a person, just as you are. You act badly sometimes, but that doesn't mean you're a bad person. If you and I were judged only on the basis of those innumerable stupid, sometimes shameful things we've done, we'd probably want to spend the rest of our lives in a closet. But I'm not writing in a closet, and I assume you're not reading in one, which means that we have been able to distinguish between ourselves as persons and the way we sometimes behave. You also extend that distinction to your friends, business associates, and even public figures. I encourage you to extend it to your stepchildren, not only for the child's good, but your own as well.

When you distinguish between the child and the child's behavior, you avoid those dangerous personality-based struggles that frustrate and defeat both you and a child. When you're admonishing a child, for example, and you get the response, "You hate me" (designed to make you feel guilty), your reply can be, "No, I don't hate you, but I hate what you're doing right now." Or when a child says something like, "You're always trying to make me feel stupid," your reponse can be, "On the contrary, I believe you're very bright. I just think you've not thought this particular problem out very carefully." When a kid does something that annoys you, your response might be, "It really annoys me when you do that," rather than, "You annoy me."

If you consistently distinguish between the child and the behavior, the child will begin to do so as well. The child begins to feel better about himself and naturally begins to behave better. As a bonus, your stepchild may begin to give you the benefit of the same distinction. Then, you'll have the makings of a relationship based on mutual respect and caring for each other as basically good people.

One of the nicest things I've ever heard was a comment from a thirteen-year-old boy about his stepfather. They had experienced several years of terrible bitterness toward each other. Then, through the stepfather's efforts to change their way of dealing with each other, their relationship began to improve. After six months, I heard the young man say, "Aw, he's not so bad. He just acts weird sometimes."

Showing (And Accepting) Affection

This book deals with the problems of stepparenting and with child management from a stepparent's perspective. One of the elements of stepparenting that is not exactly a problem, but that can often be ticklish, is the feeling and showing of affection between you and the stepchild.

The best rule of thumb about sharing affection is to let it happen, but not to force it. If you remain available and open to hugs and kisses from your stepchildren, they will proffer them when they are ready. Some natural parents insist that at least younger children make affectionate gestures to the stepparent in the hope that this will encourage harmony. Such obligatory gestures are meaningless. You'd both be better off just shaking hands or saying hello.

When you genuinely feel affectionate and want to spontaneously hug the child, go ahead and do it. The worst that can happen is that the child doesn't respond, but that's the child's problem. In any case, never insist on a show of affection from the child. Respect, yes. But genuine affection must be spontaneous to have any value.

If you and your stepchild have a habit of trading affectionate embraces when you are at home or alone together, you may be confused or hurt when the child treats you differently in the presence of his natural parents or your spouse's former mate. A stepchild inevitably has some unresolved loyalty conflicts concerning you and his natural parent. The child will have a better sense of how to treat you in the presence of the spouse you have replaced, so trust the child's instincts. If the child is old enough, talk directly with him and ask him how he'd like those situations to be handled. And, of course, never use the child's affection for you as a weapon against your mate's former spouse. In a word, let the child take the lead in affectionate behavior, while you maintain an openness to it.

Your affection for a stepchild may cause you occasional jealousy toward the other natural parent. If you must be jealous, then be jealous, but never try to interfere in the child's affection for that parent. You will not succeed, and you will damage your relationship in the process.

Chapter 6

DEALING WITH THE EX

The Best Advice

The best advice you'll ever get about dealing with your mate's ex-spouse is: Don't. If you already are: Stop. Next to the problems of dealing with stepchildren, the most harrowing difficulties come from over-involvement with ex-spouses.

Your mate's relationship with the previous spouse is an incredibly complex affair, filled with feelings, behavioral patterns, and understandings you can never hope to share. Your attempts to contribute to that relationship will benefit nobody, especially you. Even the most apparently amicable of these relationships is fraught with dangers if you get involved, and the openly hostile ones are no more or less dangerous for their angry tone.

The danger to you lies mainly in the fact that any time you become involved with the ex beyond the exchange of simple courtesies, you are, by implication, taking on responsibility for their relationship. That will almost inevitably backfire on you, no matter how noble your intentions.

The Shattered Dream

Ex-wives and ex-husbands are not bad people. You may be an ex yourself, and you're not a bad person. Your mate's ex is a person who has had an important dream shattered. She or he married at one time in an ecstasy of faith and hope, planned a future of happiness and emotional security, and had children on the basis of a deep trust in a future with your mate. It doesn't make any difference how the marriage ended or who was responsible for what. A significant portion of that dream is still intact, albeit tucked away somewhere in a subconscious corner. The more angry and hostile the ex seems to be, the more that early dream is still in force. Anger and hostility are desperate defenses against the awful pain of irrevocably broken hopes. The same holds true for your mate.

This is not an apology for bad behavior on the part of the ex (or your mate, for that matter). It is only an explanation to show what a can of worms you open if you try to involve yourself with the ex. The unalterable fact is that you have usurped the ex's dream, regardless of the intervening time or your intentions. Even if you were not involved with your mate before the divorce, you are an obstacle to the fulfillment of a dream.

The persistence of the dream and its emotional derivatives are irrational, which is why the behavior of an ex-spouse may seem irrational; yet, the behavior is consistent with the person's own perceptions and needs. Those perceptions and needs are matters you cannot be privy to. They are likely to be obscure even to the ex. This means, even if you tried, you are unlikely to achieve a mutual understanding with the ex. Without a shared understanding, effective cooperation is impossible.

Trust Requires a Common Purpose

Cooperation between people requires mutual purpose and mutual trust. By my writing this book and by your reading it, we have demonstrated a mutual purpose. We are both genuinely interested in enhancing the quality of your life as a stepparent. You trust me to honestly share with you my best judgment, based on my professional and personal experience. You may not agree with my suggestions and even choose to ignore them, but at least you have the confidence that they are meant for your benefit.

What if someone told you I was an alien from outer space bent on conquering this planet? If you were to believe that, you would wonder if we shared a mutual purpose. You would be wary of any information you accepted from me. We could not communicate effectively because the basic trust necessary for good communication would be absent.

This is essentially the nature of your relationship to your mate's ex. You place yourself in a dangerous position if you allow parts of your well-being to depend on communications between you and the ex. I'm not suggesting that you'll be deliberately lied to or mislead, although you may be. I'm saying that such communication is unlikely to have mutual purpose.

Misplaced Trust: *A Sad Example*

A young stepmother I know had met her husband about three years after his divorce. After dating for almost a year, she met his eight-year-old daughter and her already remarried mother. The mother was charming and friendly whenever they met, accommodating about visiting and travel arrangements for the daughter, and seemed delighted when an announcement was made of the impending marriage. The mother did not attend the wedding, but did send a nice gift.

When the young stepmother returned from her honeymoon, she talked frequently on the phone with the mother to check about food preferences, bedtimes, medications, and the like, so that she could be well prepared for visiting weekends to come. The mother, as always, was cordial and full of good humor, commenting upon how much her daughter looked forward to being with the stepmother. This was true, the little girl and the stepmother had a smooth, fun-filled relationship.

When the little girl arrived for her first weekend visit after the marriage, her father suggested they all go roller-skating. His daughter squealed with delight for a moment, then became very quiet and agitated, pulling the hem of her dress and biting her nails. Her dad asked what was the matter, and the girl blurted out, pointing to her new stepmother, "My mommy says I'm not supposed to go anywhere with that slut."

After the shock waves were over, the implications of that remark remained. The stepmother had believed she was developing a real friendship with the mother, and she was betrayed in that trust.

I wish I could report a quick solution to the stepmother's problem, but I can't. It only got worse. The stepmother, still believing she had a good relationship with the mother, insisted that her husband stay out of it and that she would deal with it herself. When she called to ask the mother for an explanation, the mother affected complete surprise and shock, offering only a kind of bewildered, consoling explanation that little girls sometimes had big imaginations. Mollified, the stepmother then began to question her relationship with the stepdaughter. Signs of strain began to show between them until they both dreaded visiting weekends. Meanwhile, for several months, the stepmother maintained faith in her good relationship with the mother. This misplaced faith caused her to believe the mother when the mother told her, in sad confidence, that one of the reasons she had divorced her husband was that he was sneaky and cruel, that maybe he had something to do with the little girl's behavior. It would be just like him. After the implantation of the seed of doubt, the stepmother could no longer completely trust herself, the daughter, or her husband, nobody—in fact, but the mother.

Within a year this couple was ready to divorce. The stepmother's involvement with her husband's ex had produced unbearable tensions and mistrust within the new marriage. It took nearly a year of costly therapy for them to get themselves straightened out. None of it should have been necessary.

Blatant and Subtle Sabotage

There is an interesting other side to the foregoing true story. I happened to know the ex-wife. She was, and is, a very warm, loving, thoroughly enjoyable woman who would not ordinarily deliverately hurt anybody. Her atrocious behavior toward her ex's new family was a source of deep concern to her. She knew she was damaging even her own child, but she literally could not help herself. She tried hard to curb her impulses to undermine the stepmother, but they kept getting the better of her. She was somehow compelled. She finally got herself into therapy, and she got a better control over her behavior, though not completely. From time to time she still finds herself priming her daughter to create some havoc within her daddy's marriage.

Most sabotaging and undermining are less blatant. They turn up in subtle, annoying forms. One father complained that his former wife kept moving her living quarters to more distant locations without informing him. Every four months or so, he would turn up to get his children only to find a vacant house or apartment. Having missed his weekend with his children, he would get in touch with the former wife at her office the following Monday, only to hear her complain bitterly how disappointed the children were when he did not come for them. She would always swear she remembered telling him or informing him by note of her new location.

Children Should Not Be Message Bearers

A good rule of thumb in your relations with the ex is to draw clean boundaries on the lines of communications between the people involved in these multiple family relationships. For a start, neither accept nor send information through the children. Deal directly with your mate only and with the children when they are with you. Let your mate deal with the ex.

One stepmother became angry when the children arrived for a visit with a bagful of clothes that needed laundering before being worn. The stepmother did the laundry, but in a fit of pique she told the children to tell their mother that she was not their mother's laundry service. There is no way of knowing how that message was delivered to the mother, but the result was an unholy war of nerves and dirty clothes for the next few years. Had the stepmother asked her husband to talk with his ex about the matter, the issue would have ended with the simple explanation that the mother's washing machine was on the blink that week.

Employing children to deliver messages, no matter how harmless the message might be, is dangerous for several reasons. It establishes a precedent for indirect communication between the adults involved, so that when there are sensitive communications to be handled, the children may continue to be used. You never know when a message will touch a nerve. In the case of the laundry problem, the natural mother thought the stepmother was accusing her of some dereliction of motherly duty. Dangerous business to put in the hands of children.

A couple was accustomed to asking their 14-year-old to convey to his mother the time when they would pick him up for the next weekend visit. This seemed to work well for several months until, one evening, they arrived at the specified time to find the teenager had gone off with a group of friends. His mother was fuming. The boy and his mother had been expecting the couple some three hours earlier. After much waiting and speculation, the mother allowed her son to go with his friends, believing the father was not going to appear. As it turned out, the boy had misinformed his mother, preferring to go with his friends. He had set the situation up deliberately.

Good Intentions, Bad Results

There may be a lot of discussion about everybody pulling together for the good of the children, but you may discover everyone is pulling in different directions.

If your mate and ex have one of those really bitter, terrible relationships, you may be tempted to protect your mate by dealing with the ex yourself, acting as a sort of buffer between them. That's a noble idea, but be prepared to get caught in the crunch. It is at best a thankless task, and at worst exposes you to a constant barrage of opinions about your mate that you would rather not hear. You will never be very effective in any case, because you'll never be working with complete information.

Approach your spouse's ex in about the same way you would approach the people with whom your spouse works. If your spouse has a problem with a colleague, you may well sympathize with him, but you would certainly not deal with the colleague yourself. Your spouse got involved in that relationship; let your spouse handle it.

The Peacemaker Role

You may think that your mate handles the ex with more bitterness and stubbornness than necessary. The same advice holds here. Leave your mate to handle the ex the best way he or she knows how. If your mate impresses you as being irrational when it comes to dealing with the ex, your assessment may be accurate; nevertheless, there is probably very little you can do about it. Don't make yourself unhappy trying to smooth things out.

In general, stay as removed as possible from dealing with the ex. Not because the ex is bad, but because you have no natural place in the older relationship, and your intrusion into it will only cause you trouble. You don't need it.

I am not suggesting you get mad at the ex if you aren't already. Some stepparents have excellent relationships with the ex, and you may be one of them. I do suggest, though, that you evaluate your relationship with the ex to determine if you are overinvolved. You can tell very quickly by checking your own deep feelings at the thought of dealing with the ex. If it's not a good feeling, you probably need to get a little more distance and shift more of the responsibility over to your mate.

The Green-Eyed Monster

Your mate and the ex may have a better relationship than you would like for them to have. You may find yourself being jealous of the former spouse and concerned that your mate is remaining involved with the ex beyond the apparent necessities for making arrangements about the children.

There isn't much I have to offer in helping you conquer those jealous feelings. You are in the company of tens of thousands of other second spouses. Much of the jealousy stems from your awareness that your mate and the ex have had a life of which you were not a part. While you may not want to consider it in much detail, you are aware that your spouse and the ex had years of sexual and other intimacies. They have built a basis for mutual understanding of a kind you want, but don't yet have with your mate. If this is your first marriage, you may have a difficult time accepting the prior commitments your spouse has made. Your mate and the ex are bonded, and nothing you do will sever that bond.

Unless they are actually sleeping together, in which case you should properly raise a fuss, I suggest you keep your jealous feelings to yourself. Continually challenging your mate's relationship with the ex will probably only drive it underground, creating even more worry and bad feelings for yourself. It is not unusual for formerly married folks with children to check in with each other quite often, and they may still love each other in a special kind of way. But that does not necessarily diminish your mate's commitment to you. Leave their relationship alone. You'll only get burned.

Visitation Schedules and The Ex

Many ex-spouses exert, or try to exert, control of stepparented families by making demands about how the children are to be handled. The most obvious of these ploys is a stringent, unworkable visitation schedule for the children.

A father I know was a student working part-time when he divorced. He worked out a visitation schedule with his two children whereby he would pick them up from school three nights a week, keep them until 10:00 p.m., and deliver them to his former wife on his way to work. In addition, he would have them each Saturday. The schedule worked out well for him and the children, as well as his ex-wife, as long as he was in school and single. In his last year of graduate school, he got married, and soon after he got a regular nine-to-five job. His former wife was very bitter about his remarriage.

For a year, three nights a week, the new stepmother picked up the children from school, having to leave her own job early on those days. Her husband would not return home from delivering the children until well after eleven. By that time, they were both too tired to spend any productive time together. Because they had the children every Saturday, they could not make plans for a full weekend, and the ex would not hear of any deviation from the schedule. That schedule was distorting this new couple's entire life.

The husband was reluctant to change the schedule because he was afraid the children would be hurt. He was still feeling tremendously guilty about the children, and he was loathe to upset their schedule for fear he would lose them altogether. The ex-wife was adept at playing on his guilt. Meanwhile, the marriage was about to break up.

By the end of the year, the stepmother would take no more of it. She put her foot down and demanded that he sue for a change in visitation to every other weekend. The father, through professional counseling, overcame his guilt feelings and decided that the children would survive a change in visitation. He sued for a change, and the ex fought, knowing she would lose control of her former husband if he won. The court granted his request. For the stepmother, the result was a normalization of her marriage and a significant decrease in her resentment toward the children. At last report, things were going well between the father and his new wife, the children were fine, and the ex was still bitter.

Changing Visitation Schedules

Most visitation schedules are worked out at the time of the divorce and may have made sense at that time. Since you have married, though, you and your spouse are in the process of developing a lifestyle of your own, and the visitation schedule may have become unnecessarily burdensome. If you find your lifestyle is being dominated by the visitation schedule, do what you can to get your spouse to change it to something more workable. If the presence of your stepchildren is interrupting your life in an unreasonable way, you will likely begin to resent them. A change in visitation schedule will not harm the children unduly, and you will eliminate an important element of the former spouse's control over your life.

Setting Your Own Child Management Policies

Another way former spouses try to exert control over your family is by insisting you treat the children in certain ways. The unwary stepparent can easily fall into the trap of agreeing to abide by the ex's methods of handling the children. This happens mainly when you have the children only on visits, but it is a dangerous precedent to set. Some natural parents insist you abide by their systems of handling things like bedtimes, prayers, eating habits, methods of discipline, restriction from certain activities, follow-up on punishments begun by the parent, and so on. I know one mother who insisted that, if the child were to live with the father and stepmother for the summer, the stepmother would have to quit her job and stay home with the child.

Except for things like medication schedules, you and your spouse will do well to set your own child management policies. If those policies match the desires of the ex, so much the better, but don't try to duplicate the child's environment with the custodial parent. Unless your spouse is under a court order to abide by certain wishes of the ex, quietly but firmly deal with your stepchildren in the way that works best for you and your spouse. The argument that children must be treated consistently by all adults caring for them is false. Children learn to deal with adults much as you do. They learn your personality and expectations for them, and they adapt themselves accordingly. This is a healthful growth-producing part of their up-bringing.

You can be sure your stepchild will report any inconsistencies of treatment to the custodial parent, sometimes gloating that you are more lenient, sometimes complaining that you are more strict. That doesn't concern you. Your responsibility is to yourself and your family. You'll drive yourself to distraction trying to handle your stepchildren exactly as the custodial parent does. Don't even try. If conflicts arise about general management, let your mate handle them. You stick to your own best judgment.

If you have no natural children of your own, you may be a little intimidated by the custodial spouse and sometimes wish to turn to him or her for advice on how to deal with the children. That's a natural desire, and on occasions it is necessary. Eventually, however, you will have to forge your own relationship with the stepchildren. In the long run, you may be better off getting needed advice from your spouse or from a friend with children. It isn't that your spouse's ex will give you bad advice, it's only that the advice is likely to be biased.

Chapter 7

LAUGHING MATTERS

Nothing will serve the cause of a satisfying step-relationship better than a sense of humor. If you are good at cracking jokes, crack some. If you can't remember a joke for three minutes, learn the trick of turning your attention to the silliest aspect of things.

Humor Slays Goliath

I talked with a woman whose whole day had been focused on a desperate struggle with a ten-year-old who refused to take some garbage cans from the garage to the curb. After demanding, screaming, and bitter name-calling, she sat in her kitchen thoroughly unnerved. On a doodle pad she noticed that she had been absent-mindedly tracing her stepchild's name, David. Underneath, the word g-o-l-i-a-t-h began to form, trailing off the page in defeat. She was suddenly filled with a sense of how ludicrous her battle was with this child.

Going to the foot of the stairs, she called up to the child in his room, "The Philistines surrender and retreat, your champion is too well armed, and my head is valuable to me." David didn't understand the allusion, but a half hour later he crept from his room to find his stepmother humming while she potted plants.

"What are you doing?" he asked belligerently.

"Potting plants on the banks of the Red Sea and planning my next attack," she said.

"Huh?" said he, but she returned to her plants. Fifteen minutes later the scrape of metal on concrete told her the war was over.

Dressed For Battle

Thirty-four-year-old Al Moore had a hostile relationship with his fifteen-year-old stepson. The previous night the boy had come in very late, blind drunk. Al's stomach was in knots for the morning confrontation. Then he came up with an idea.

147

In the morning, while the sullen boy was draped on the couch watching cartoons, Al suddenly appeared wearing a football helmet and shoulder pads, a boxing glove on one hand, and a baseball bat in the other. Standing in front of the TV, Al said, "We are not going to have this conversation," and left the room as quickly as he had entered. On each subsequent occasion when the boy stepped out of bounds, Al repeated the procedure. One day the boy turned up in Al's workshop clad in the same outrageous outfit. He said, "Al, this is dumb."

"Right you are," said Al, "Help me move this motor, will you?"

The relationship improved greatly.

A Pundamental Solution

On the weekends when her husband's three children came to visit, Ellen invariably found herself tense. The headaches would start on Thursday, stomach problems at noon on Friday. She sometimes had visions of being trapped in the type of crushing machine used for junk cars. When the children arrived, Ellen would numbly go through the motions of greeting, feeding, cleaning, and riding in a car packed with people.

There was nothing she could pinpoint as a cause for her malaise. The children were not badly behaved; in fact, they seemed to like her and treated her well. Her husband knew what was happening to her, for she had explained her feelings to him, but he was at a loss to understand the cause or come up with a solution. After two years of suffering through such weekends, she didn't think she could stand another.

Ellen's sense of humor was not a great one, but she had a knack for making puns. In desperation, she decided she would concentrate on making a pun of anything that came to hand. One Friday evening, just before he went to get the children, her husband asked how she was feeling. She replied, "I'm in the present tense." No belly laughs, but an appreciative chuckle from both of them. When one of the children offered to fill the ice cube trays, she said, "That would be nnn-ice." When the seven-year-old girl broke a glass and cut her toe, Ellen remarked that the girl was a real cut-up. Throughout the weekend Ellen came up with some good ones (and some very bad ones).

The children caught on and a two-day contest developed. The twelve-year-old brought her a baseball, and with a facetiously sad countenance he reported it was all "bat-tered." The nine-year-old surprised everyone with her command of the language. After unsuccessfully searching for something to wear to church, she said, "I guess

I just can't skirt the issue." Even the normally very sober husband commented on the change in atmosphere with a quiet statement on their way home from returning the children to their mother. "Well," he said, "when in doubt, punn-t."

The gambit paid off handsomely. During the ensuing years the game has continued in various forms and has opened new areas of fun for the family. The oldest boy, now in college, turned up unexpectedly one recent weekend, specifically to stage an elaborate, pun-filled performance for Ellen's benefit. He was comfortable in coming, and she was glad to have him.

Humor Reveals The Brighter Side of Ourselves

Humor is often a matter of carrying a situation to its ridiculous extremes. It need not produce big laughs; it need only take the edge off the seriousness of a situation.

Humor reduces the proportions of our problems. It reminds us that nothing is worth the sacrifice of our joy of living. Life is short. Problems in relationships are episodic; they come and go. They become oppressive only when they are allowed to preempt the good features of a relationship.

Humor helps us put things into perspective. It reveals the incongruities and absurdities of our existence. No problem between two people remains a problem long if they both can laugh at it.

The Sense In Nonsense

Mary is a stepmother who describes herself as having little sense of humor. She is a lovely person, but try as she may, she finds nothing particularly amusing. Anecdotes and jokes only perplex her. I believe she has never laughed, and for this I am sorry for her. On the other hand, she is gifted with an ability for logical thinking and a kind of contented resignation to the inconsistencies of life.

Mary has developed a remarkably successful method of coping with day-to-day difficulties. When she has a conflict with another person, she asks herself: "What could be the worst possible outcome of this conflict?" She will then conjure up a ridiculous series of consequences, one leading to the next. As she does, there is inevitably a point where the consequences become unbelievable, and the absurdity takes the edge off the intensity of the situation.

She has an eleven-year-old stepdaughter who had been refusing to practice her piano lessons. The struggle between them had become a source of very bad feelings. Mary, the stepmother, approached it this way:

"Joannie," she began, "if I send you to your room as a punishment, you will not be able to practice. If I spank you, your bottom will be sore and you'll not be able to sit on the piano bench. So, neither of those solutions is any good. However, you must practice because, if you don't, you'll become a very poor piano player. You may be playing on television one day, and you'll play so poorly some people may turn off their TV's. And if they turn off their TV's, they may not see the tornado warnings just after your performance. Since they've missed the warnings, their houses may be destroyed and some of them may even be hurt. One of them might even be an ambulance driver. Then he could neither help himself nor anyone else. Many people would suffer. So, instead of entertaining people with music, you may cause a great disaster. That would not be good, I'm sure you agree. Please go ahead and practice for a half hour, then you may go out and play."

The weaving of this scenario shifted the focus of their struggle from whether Joannie was going to practice to whether Mary's story was credible. Mary carried the situation beyond its present importance to a ridiculous extreme, forcing Joannie to employ her own sense of humor in appreciating the scenario itself. When Joannie replied with, "Aw, come on, Mary, that's not going to happen," Mary agreed it might not.

Mary then launched into another, similarly ridiculous scenario, one delighting Joannie even more. The structure of their relationship changed with the conversation, at least temporarily, and the power struggle was over. Joannie gave up her sutborn refusal to practice the piano.

Even if Joannie had continued to refuse the practice, Mary would have removed herself from the struggle. Ironically, Mary had tried to describe the problem as leading to the end of the world, but her treatment of the description took on a ridiculous aspect. Thus, it became apparent to her that the worst that could happen had manageable proportions.

Digging for Buried Humor

The purpose of a sense of humor is to dissipate the immediacy and intensity of a situation, to divert energy in harmless directions. A useful technique is to comment directly on your perception of the relationship at the moment and to speculate about its outcome. "We sure are mad at each other right now. I suppose we'll end up breaking each other's arms. Then, there we'll be, side by side in the hospital, having a contest to see who can get the most signatures on her cast."

This sort of thing is not humor in a Ha Ha sense, of course, but it lightens intensity and adds an awareness of a future to your relationship with the child. I heard an astute stepfather say to a thirteen-year-old, "I sure hope we get this settled before our canoe trip this weekend; I don't think I'd survive all the dunkings you'd put me through." That statement identified for the boy, and the man as well, the certainty of a future relationship that still contained expectations of some fun and good-natured relations.

There is almost no situation that doesn't have some comical element to it, if you will look for it. Can you imagine how a political cartoonist would depict your being driven from your house by a five-year-old? Even your sarcastic appreciation of such a thing gives you a better perspective. Can you picture yourself as the wicked stepmother in Hansel and Gretel? Look in the mirror; there's no resemblance. Can you imagine yourself as David Copperfield's stepfather, stealing his wife's property and driving David penniless from his home? You're not that evil. Nothing is as bad as it seems. If you will consistently use your own good sense of humor, you will take yourself and your situation less seriously, and you'll be doing everyone a favor. Especially yourself.

When you're in a conflict with another person, give your temper a chance to cool a little. Shift the basis of your interacting to something else. The problem will not go away. It will patiently wait while you take a breather. This is the opportunity to look for a little humor.

Maybe, just maybe, a touch of unexpected humor can change the mood, the perspective, and the emphasis to loosen up the grimmest deadlock.

Children May Provide The Best Laugh

Children respond to a sense of humor even when they don't understand it. They are quick to catch on to the spirit of humor, and, if you're attentive, they will amaze you with their comic talents. If you're not too wrapped up in yourself, you can get a good laugh from them.

A stepmother of my acquaintance plays a game with herself and her stepchildren called, "I Am Perfect In Every Way." Having failed to get the children to clean up their room at her first request, she stands in the bedroom doorway and addresses them thusly: "Children, as you know, I am perfect in every way. And, of course, so are you. But there is a word gobbler in this house who ate every word I said when I made it perfectly clear you were supposed to clean up your room. If you had heard me, since you are perfect, you would have done it right away. I just can't imagine where that word gobbler came from."

Usually that little speech, or one like it, has

the desired effect. One morning, though, the ten-year-old raised himself up to his most dramatic height and responded: "Alice, as you know, we are perfect in every way. We have invented the perfect word gobbler."

Laughter Despite All

When all else fails, force yourself to laugh. When the tension is so bad that you expect to cry, when you feel that there is no escape from your myriad problems, when you're so outraged you could scream, force yourself to laugh. The harder the better. People will think you're crazy if you do it in a public place. Get into your car, then, and find a long, quiet, safe stretch of road. There, far from the crowd, force yourself to laugh. If at first you can only sob and cry, fine, you need to do that too. But keep trying to laugh. Just go through the physical motions of laughing until it takes over on its own. It will. Once you're laughing, continue until you're exhausted and your cheeks hurt and your sides ache. You don't have to laugh at anything in particular. Just laugh. When you do, I promise that the world will look much better to you.

Chapter 8

EMOTIONAL HEALTH OF THE CHILD

The Emotional Nature of Children

Children are remarkable people. Their imagination and curiosity seem bondless, and they have the ability to engross themselves in activites to the exclusion of almost everything else. Most children see themselves at the very center of the universe. In the exuberance of their imaginations, they can create worlds for themselves; worlds as real and vital as the one we adults live in, but usually much more interesting.

Children have a finely tuned instinct for adaptability and survival. The younger they are, the less they are influenced by the intellectually and emotionally deadening customs of adults. They think and act in ways that meet their needs without concern for the social restraints that adults saddle themselves with.

Most of all, children have intensity of spirit. They allow themselves freedom to be absolutely delighted or completely devastated. While we adults systematically flatten our lives to dull moderation, children stimulate their lives by seeking the topmost peaks and deepest depths of human emotional experience. Is it any wonder children some times balk at our attempts to channel their spirit within the narrow limits of our adult expectations? Psychological theory notwithstanding, I think the real reason most of us adults have trouble remembering our childhood is embarrassment at having abandoned our search for fulfilling excitement.

The Three Necessities

Nevertheless, children need to be brought into the world in which we live. As a stepparent, you know you will exert some influence on your stepchildren, and you'll naturally want to do what is best for them.

There are only three things children really need. First they need food and shelter from the elements until they can provide their own.

Second, they need to love and be loved by at least one other person. Third, they need to learn how to think for themselves.

You can help provide part of their food and shelter needs, and you can help teach them how to think for themselves. If you can develop a bonded, loving relationship with a stepchild, fine; however a child should not have to rely on you for that particular need to be fulfilled.

Emotional Coddling

During the 1960s and since, there has been a national obsession with the psychological welfare of children. Many mental health and education professionals have come to the conclusion that anything that causes emotional distress in a child is to be avoided at all cost. Adults are convinced that divorce in a family is almost certain to land the children in psychiatric hospitals. School systems bend over backwards, even eliminating academic requirements, to ensure that children never suffer the distress of failure. They teach that feelings are more important than achievement. For the past two decades, children have been told that they are not responsible for what they do, but that their parents are. Such foolishness.

If you have grown up during the last twenty years and have this attitude toward children, you're probably worried about the psychological implications of whatever you're doing with your stepchildren. Let me set some of your fears to rest.

Children Are Adaptable

Children of divorced families have no higher incidence of serious mental health problems than children from conventional homes. Faced with the necessity for adaptation, children are much more adept at managing tough emotional situations than are adults. You, as a stepparent, would have to go well out of your way, by deliberate design, to psychologically damage a child.

Children Must Be Able To Achieve

To train a child that feeling and expression of feelings are the only bases for his value as a human being, to minimize the importance of personal accomplishment, is to deny the child the only way in which he really can feel good about himself. High self-regard comes from the successful negotiation of conflict situations and from using one's own intellect to garner information and to make judgments in his own behalf.

Children, at all ages, need to have the opportunity to both succeed and fail. Only by testing their capabilities can they measure their capabilities.

A Child Must Be Able To Decide

The adult's responsibility is to create realistic conditions under which the children may test themselves. By realistic, I mean you wouldn't expect a four-year-old to make a decision about the relative merits of capitalism versus communism. On the other hand, you might well expect a four-year-old to judge for himself whether it is better to keep what is his or to give it away on the demand of a sibling.

Dealing with children of any age is never very easy, but it becomes even more difficult if you make most of their decisions for them. You undoubtedly have values and attitudes that you believe would be good for the child to adopt. Nothing is wrong with explaining and exemplifying those values in the hope the child will adopt them; however, a child must ultimately come to terms with the values and attitudes that suit him as an individual. You produce little but unnecessary conflict when you insist too hard on an acceptance of your beliefs.

Occasionally you must stand by and watch a child, of any age, struggle and sweat over a decision that to you is obvious. If you make the decision yourself and impose it on the child, the child only comes to believe he never has to make decisions on his own. This does not mean you allow children to make decisions that could lead to harm. You can set limits on choices available to a child, depending on your assessment of the child's ability to handle certain kinds of problems. Within those limits, however, the child should be allowed to make mistakes, even if you know they will cause the child embarrassment or other discomfort.

Praising Decision-Making, If Not The Decision

The ten-year-old daughter of a very successful young stepmother I know was preparing to go to her first birthday party. In spite of the stepmother's objection, the little girl insisted on wearing an outfit that the stepmother knew would be inappropriate. The little girl returned home well before the party ended, in tears, saying she had been too embarrassed to stay at the party dressed as she was. This wise stepmother's response was to praise the girl for having made some decisions on her own and to offer to be a consultant in the future. The stepmother was careful not to denigrate the child's decision-making ability by saying, "I told you so." The little girl learned a great deal more from that episode than she would have if the stepmother had forced her opinion on the girl.

The Child's View of Divorce

Although most children do not suffer serious emotional damage from their parents' divorce, all children are nevertheless affected. The time required for children to come to terms with the trauma varies greatly from child to child; some never do. For a child, coming to terms with divorce means the child accepts the reality of the divorce; that is, the child comes to understand and believe that the parents are not going to live together again or raise the child as husband and wife. Beyond that acceptance, the critical factor in the successful negotiation of the trauma is the ability to maintain a productive relationship with both natural parents.

"It's All My Fault"

Many children develop a belief that they are responsible for their parents' separation and divorce. They heap terrible guilt upon themselves for a decision made by their parents. How they come to that belief will vary with each child, but a typical situation occurs when the strains just prior to a separation between the parents make the parents tense and irritable. They often take some of that tension out on the child. The child finds himself being criticized and punished beyond normal proportion to his misdeed, which leads him to think that he must be really bad. When the separation between his parents actually takes place, the child may be convinced that his bad behavior caused the break.

The parents have the responsibility to assure a child that the decision to divorce is entirely theirs, that the divorce has nothing to do with the child's behavior. Even so, these assurances are often not accepted. A child may have an emotional stake in the belief that his parents are infallible. The child may prefer to take responsibility upon himself rather than to admit to himself that either or both parents could make such a terrible mistake.

The Arbitrator

The depth of a child's conviction as to his level of responsibility is often a measure of how hard the child tries to get his parents back together. In the child's logic, if he is responsible for the divorce, then he must also be responsible for patching up the marriage. A child holding this belief requires firm, constant reassurance that he is not responsible for the divorce and that the parents are not going to reunite under any circumstances.

Contention Over The Child's Loyalty

Maintaining productive relationships with both natural parents is often made tremendously difficult for a child because of the respective parents' attitudes toward one another. Nothing is so sad or viciously irresponsible as the employment of children as conscriptees in the hateful wars between divorcing adults. Some parents disgracefully demand that their children in one way or another abandon their relationship with the other natural parents. The demand is not only disgraceful, but it is impossible to fulfill, for children are irrevocably bonded to both natural parents.

Even under the best of circumstances, a child must forge new patterns of relating to both parents after a divorce. This is no easy task, for even if the parents are not placing loyalty demands on the child, the child may be struggling with loyalty issues on his own. Forging new patterns of relationship with a divorced parent requires time, sometimes several years, until both the child and the parent become comfortable with each other.

Enter The Stepparent

As a stepparent, you represent an added dimension to the child's problem of learning to deal with the natural parent you have married. Both your mate and the children have a lot of tough work to do as they find new ways of dealing with each other. They will make shocking, painful mistakes with each other as they grow into a new relationship. Your wisest course is to be sensitive to their struggles, but when you feel compelled to protect either your mate or the children from themselves, contain yourself. Your involvement in their affairs is not likely to be productive in the long run and will almost inevitably add to their difficulties. Most children eventually adapt to their parents' divorce and its implications, including you, but they have to do it in their own way to be successful.

During the period of adaptation, the children are bound to undergo emotional pain and conflict. You will encounter some tough behavioral problems connected with the process. This does not necessarily mean the child is emotionally damaged; it mainly means the child is going through difficult processes of problem solving. During these processes the child learns a great deal about himself, his natural parents, and the world around him.

Common Sense In Judging Emotional Behavior

For the last twenty years or so, you've been subjected to a lot of popular psychology regarding the needs of children. Much of it suggests that you are not really fit to deal properly with them. Mental health professionals, like myself, who deal with children with serious psychological or emotional disorders, have as a group, spent the last twenty years scaring you into thinking that we are the only ones who know how to handle children. That's nonsense. The incidence of emotional disorders in children is very slight. The truth is that anyone with a little common sense will do just fine raising children.

For the most part, trust your instincts. You are as capable as anyone else of judging whether the emotional and behavioral climate you and your spouse are setting for the children is one that promotes the way you want them to be and act. As mentioned before, children are not easily psychologically damaged; in fact, they are incredibly versatile and adaptable. They are also incredibly adept at making unwary adults worry. If you and your spouse have a good idea about what you want to accomplish on behalf of a child, and you move toward those goals with a firm good will, you need not worry much about his psychological and emotional development. That will pretty much take care of itself.

Detecting Serious Emotional Disturbance

Be very careful about confusing a child's entirely normal distress and occasionally unacceptable behavior with serious emotional disturbance. It would be abnormal for a child not to have some problems with the divorce of his parents and with your marriage to one of them. You may well bear the brunt of some hostility; if so, simply let the child know that you understand that he or she is angry about something. Unless the child wants to talk about it, leave it alone.

If you do have a child who is emotionally disturbed, you'll know it. Using your own emotional antennae, you can feel, as well as observe, serious emotional disturbances in a child. There is a significant difference between behavior problems and emotional disturbance. A serious emotional disturbance is normally the concern of the natural parents who should see about getting professional help.

There is a simple and effective way for you to determine if your stepchild is developing within normal limits. Visit a day care center or school that handles children the same age as your stepchild. Sit in the classrooms, stand in the halls, hang around the playgrounds, and observe. You don't even need to talk to anybody, just let your impressions of the general behavior and emotional tone of the children flow through you. Watch how they play, how they study, how they interact with each other.

When you see a group of children in the course of their daily lives, you'll get an accurate enough sense of whether your stepchild is operating within acceptable tolerances of growth and development. Observe children both a year older and younger than your stepchild, as well. Children develop at their own pace, and a year at either end of the median is usually within acceptable limits.

This exercise will also give you a valuable insight into what your stepchild's life is really like. Your experience with a child is usually limited to interactions within your home, and this is a small part of a child's total experience. If you feel you need more detailed information on the development of children, go to the library and get any of Jean Piaget's books. He has done more than anyone else to influence current thinking and understanding of how and why children develop the way they do.

No Excuse For Bad Behavior

Emotional distress does not excuse unacceptable behavior. That would only teach the child that it's all right to act out of line if he feels bad or is angry.

I'm not suggesting you be inattentive to children's feelings. They are people whose feelings deserve respect and attention like anyone else's. I am suggesting, however, that you be careful about letting a child get away with behavior that unduly upsets your own life just because the child has a cause for emotional distress.

You As An Outsider From Their Emotional Lives

Be aware that your stepchildren have no natural relationship to you. You are in their lives because of a choice made by one of their natural parents. If they do not choose to confide in you or share their thoughts and feelings with you, don't worry that something is wrong with either them or you. Whenever you would like to have them treat you as a parent or confidant, remember that they have no real reason to do so.

You are, and may remain, just another adult in their lives, one whom they have no natural desire to get close to or trust. No matter what you and your spouse tell them, they are unlikely to really believe your marriage is going to last. They have already seen their natural parents divorce. Why should they believe your marriage will be any different?

They may, indeed, deeply resent your presence in their parent's life, seeing you as an obstacle to the reuniting of their real mother and father. When this is the case, you can expect them to have little willingness to get close to you; in fact, they may do their level best to drive you out. Your best approach is to let them know that you understand their feelings, but that you still expect them to behave appropriately.

You As A Figure Of Respect

Your stepchildren may never love you, but if you maintain a posture of firm good will and clear behavioral expectations toward them, they will ultimately have no choice but to respect you. A stepfather of my acquaintance tried for two years to get his stepchildren to like him. Finally he changed his posture and developed a comfortable relationship with the children. He told me that he remembered a teacher he had in high school with whom he had a very difficult time. This teacher had very high expectations and insisted that his students meet them. Nobody in school liked that teacher, until later, when the teacher was about the only one any of the students remembered with any real appreciation or affection. You have a teacher like that in your background; perhaps you can learn something from that teacher's methods.

Summary

Children are resilient, adaptable, and able to cope with almost anything if they understand they must. You can be most helpful to a child by creating an atmosphere of warmth and good will and by helping the child feel good about himself through achievement and decision-making. I urge you not to worry too much about his mental health. When you have a child experiencing some emotional stress, be available to the extent you are comfortable, but avoid trying to play therapist. By all means, do not allow unacceptable behavior on the basis of that stress.

In the rare case that a child's behavior gets too far out of hand as a result of emotional strain, suggest that your mate get some professional help. For the most part, though, leave the emotional struggles of your stepchildren and your mate to themselves for resolution.

Afterword

In this book, I have identified many of the common problems of stepparenting and have suggested possible solutions. I have also tried to show you how to resolve problems peculiar to you and your family. I believe that this matter-of-fact approach is best for stepparents who are serious about improving their lives. An unfortunate consequence of this approach is that it tends to present stepparenting as a gloomy, problem-infested style of life. It doesn't make stepparenting seem like much fun.

In reality, stepparenting can be a tremendously rewarding experience for those who do it well. Most stepparents, after an initial period of conflicts, develop good communication skills with stepchildren and the natural parents. They acquire the knack of clearly identifying and accepting appropriate roles. They find stepparenting a uniquely satisfying way of challenging and testing their own potentials for personal growth and achievement of human intimacy.

Marriages involving stepchildren allow much more freedom of choice in how one relates to the other family members. Since there is no socially prescribed role for a stepparent, the stepparent has the opportunity to create a special relationship that suits the mutual needs of his or her own life and the life of the stepchildren.

As a stepparent, you may see your challenges as problems to be worried over, or as opportunities for your own growth as a person. If you can see them as creative challenges, then the rewards for meeting them are great, and you acquire a bit of greatness for having met them.

Many of the ideas and suggestions contained in this book are useful for improving other aspects of your life. For example, dealing with in-laws, friends, and co-workers can become more satisfying if you use some of the same principles and techniques you have learned in your struggles as a stepparent. As a rule, anything that works well for you in one human situation will probably work well in others.

If there is a single wish I have for you, it is that you will be gentle with yourself. Life is too precious to waste in worry and self-deprecation. There is unbelievable beauty in the dance of family life, if you will but attend to the music and forgive the occasional stumbles.